PRINCESS DIANA

DIAGNOSED

PSYCHOLOGICAL DIAGNOSIS

OF HER SECRET LIFE

Dr. Paul Dawson

VISTAR BOOKS

Published by Vistar Pictures, Ltd.

PRINCESS DIANA DIAGNOSED

PSYCHOLOGICAL DIAGNOSIS OF HER SECRET LIFE

REVISED: October 28th, 2020

Copyright © 2020 by Dr. Paul Dawson

Dr. Paul Dawson's **PRINCESS DIANA DIAGNOSED: PSYCHOLOGICAL DIAGNOSIS OF HER SECRET LIFE** presents a new analysis of the enigmatic, mysterious fairy-tale Princess – diagnosing her by an in-depth assessment of her secret life. Diana's family, early life, royal celebrity, lovers, relationships, marriage, and mental condition is scrutinized.

Here, revealed are Diana's mental disorders that include her bulimia (overeating then self-induced vomiting); self-mutilation (cutting herself out of guilt or depression). Was she a pathological liar? Did Princess Diana have a twisted and confused identity disorder? Why did Diana plunge into a series of tawdry and secretive love-sex affairs? A must-read for any fan of the world's most famous royal Princess.

Princess Diana called Dr. Dawson at his New York home in January 1996. He was expecting her call because a woman client of his, Victoria (nom de plume), who was a good friend of Diana, had referred Dr. Dawson to her. His New York client, Victoria, who was seeing him for individual psychotherapy, was a socialite with political connections, was famous as an international jet setter, and often socialized with European royalty, the rich and famous.

Early in 1996, Victoria and Dr. Dawson flew by private jet to London, met with Princess Diana at Victoria's mansion in the London area, and scheduled psychotherapy sessions in person with Diana for several months.

Dr. Dawson earned a Ph.D. in clinical psychology from The New School for Social Research, Graduate Faculty in New York City. He has been a psychologist in clinics, schools, and mental hospitals. Dr. Dawson was a chief psychologist of a state prison system. He has been in private practice & consulting in New York; he has written over 60 books.

PRINCESS DIANA DIAGNOSED

PSYCHOLOGICAL DIAGNOSIS OF HER SECRET LIFE

BOOK REVIEWS:

Melodie Heisler

*****(*5.0 out of 5 stars*) **Informative!**
Reviewed in the United States on October 3, 2014
Very informative, as is his latest book on Diana (<u>Princess Diana's Therapist</u>). I have been recommending them to various people around the world.

Amberry

*****(*5.0 out of 5 stars*) **Five Stars!**
Reviewed in the United States on January 28, 2015
Verified Purchase
Great reading!

Reviewer

*****(*5.0 out of 5 stars*) **Princess Diana gets a psychological evaluation! Highest recommendation.**
Reviewed in the United States on August 22, 2019
Verified Purchase
Dr. Dawson did a captivating psychological evaluation of Princess Diana. At last, a clinical psychologist reveals the real Princess Diana. Fabulous read. Captivating.

BOOKS BY DR. PAUL DAWSON:

BIPOLAR ZOO; BIPOLAR JUNGLE; BORDERLINE PERSONALITY DISORDER; BPD RECOVERY; CHARACTER INTELLIGENCE (CI); CAMPUS KILLER'S SECRET OBSESSION; CULT GIRLS; GRACE KELLY SESSIONS; GRACE KELLY IN THERAPY; HOW TO GET SOBER; JACKIE IN PSYCHOANALYSIS; JACKIE O SESSIONS; JACKIE ONASSIS IN THERAPY; JFK JR MURDERED; JODI ARIAS; MANSON FAMILY MANUAL; MANSON INTERVIEWS RAW; MARILYN MONROE DIAGNOSED; MASKS OF A LADY KILLER; MASKS of PREDATORS; MASKS of SEX PREDATORS; MASKS of TED BUNDY; MY PRINCESS DIANA THERAPY SESSIONS; MY TED BUNDY INTERVIEWS RAW!; MARILYN MURDERED; NARCOTERRORIST PSYCHOPATHS; PRINCESS DIANA DIAGNOSED; PRINCESS DIANA PSYCHOLOGICAL DIAGNOSIS; PRINCESS DIANA'S THERAPIST; PSYCHOLOGY OF HIDDEN INFLUENCE; PSYCHOLOGY of MEN WHO ABUSE WOMEN; PSYCHOPATHS; ROCK STARS DIAGNOSED; ROYAL SESSIONS; ROYAL SESSIONS 2; ROYAL SESSIONS 3; ROYALS THERAPIST; ROYALS THERAPIST 2; SERIAL KILLERS; SERIAL KILLERS 2; SERIAL KILLERS 3; SEX CRIMES; SEX, LOVE & SMART DATING; SKULL SCRAPERS: A CAMILLE LAURENT THRILLER (series of ten thriller novels); SPIES & ASSASSINS; SPIRITUAL THERAPY; TED BUNDY'S SEX LIFE; TERRORIST IMPERATIVE; THE MASKS OF KARLA HOMOLKA.

PRINCESS DIANA DIAGNOSED

PSYCHOLOGICAL DIAGNOSIS

OF HER SECRET LIFE

Table of Contents

WARNING: GRAPHIC CONTENT

PROLOGUE

Princess Diana called me at my New York home in January 1996. I was expecting her call because a woman client of mine, Victoria (nom de plume), who was a good friend of Diana, had referred me to her. My New York client, Victoria, who was seeing me for individual psychotherapy, was a socialite with political connections, was famous as an international jet setter, and often socialized with European royalty, the rich and famous.

Early in 1996, Victoria and I flew by private jet to London, met with Princess Diana at Victoria's mansion in the London area, and scheduled psychotherapy sessions in person with Diana for several months.

Dr. Dawson: I'm ready to work if you want to share what's on your mind.

Princess Diana: I've fallen in love with a man named Eaton Sterling (pseudonym). He frequently travels away from London on business, finance, investments. He's closing some business deal. Eaton called me this afternoon from Paris.

Pictured are Diana's lovers: Cavalryman James Hewitt, rugby star Will Carling and bodyguard Barry Mannakee.

Dr. Dawson: And something happened in Paris to disturb you.

Princess Diana: He had lunch with his daughter Claire who's attending college in Paris. Claire's been working on Eaton to reconcile with his wife, Olivia. Eaton's separated from Olivia and promised me it's over. Now he's talking about moving back in with Olivia to make Claire happy. I was hurt and then furious. I'm not interested in a triangle. I told him no sex, no relationship unless it was over with Olivia. I'm feeling used again.

Dr. Dawson: Again?

Princess Diana: Yes. Again.

Dr. Dawson: (I looked at my notes on Diana's bio timeline.) I've heard some names in the media: Barry Mannakee 1987, James Hewitt 1991, Oliver Hoare 1992, James Gilbey 1994, Will Carling 1994, and Dr. Hasnat Khan 1995. Didn't you just make a recent trip to Pakistan related to Hasnat Khan?

Pictured are Diana's lovers: PR executive James Gilbey, art dealer Oliver Hoare, and Hasnat Khan.

Princess Diana: Oh my god! I sound like a sexual predator. You can divide stories in the media into "Princess Diana the sex slut" and "Princess Di, the angel, out saving the world." Don't forget my spouse.

Dr. Dawson: You're still separated from him, aren't you? Why don't you start by telling me the story of each man starting with Prince Charles? Maybe we can see if there is a pattern. Then if you try something different, you might get different results.

Princess Diana: By the way, I'm working on divorcing Charles. Do you want me to start with my childhood?

Dr. Dawson: Not now. We can get to that later as it comes up. Let's start with the significant others – the men from your love life starting with Prince Charles. Correct me if I'm wrong, but you first met Prince Charles when you were 16-years-old at Althorp in 1977?

Princess Diana: I need to frame this in a historical context. In hindsight, after 20 years of experience and education, I might have turned Prince Charles down and said no to his marriage proposal.

Princess Diana was a fashion icon. Have Meghan and Kate taken notes?

In retrospection, I now realize that I was something of a victim of sexual politics that were threatening the monarchy. In the 1960s, royalty did not handle well the sexual revolution.

Dr. Dawson: How so?

Princess Diana: The feminist revolution left most of the "appropriate" (quotes with her fingers) or eligible single young women in the royal orbit with a "past," a "history," and "experienced" – meaning they were no longer virgins.

Dr. Dawson: Young women were coming down off their pedestals that men put them on. Am I right?

Princess Diana: They were not only not virgins but also had enough experiences to have judgment, shrewdness, wisdom, and opinions.

Women changing, advancing, was repulsive to the monarchy establishment that had conditioned Prince Charles to seek a virgin bride to be Princess of Wales.

Prince Harry fears his wife, Meghan Markle, will be hounded by the paparazzi like Princess Diana was.

Dr. Dawson: And, of course, Charles went along with the program.

Princess Diana: Prince Philip and Lord "Dickie" Mountbatten had coached Charles. They urged him to sew his wild oats, screw as many girls as humanly possible. Then marry a noble virgin bride who would be submissive and obedient. And guess what? Have your sexual affairs on the side, such as with good old Camilla. And I do mean old.

Dr. Dawson: Why did Prince Charles propose marriage to you?

Princess Diana: Prince Charles picked me because I was a naïve virgin from the aristocratic and royal class. My role was to be a lump of clay to be shaped into filling the role of a royal princess.

My opinions and perceptions were not wanted. Charles did not love me. It was just a royal duty to find a wife and have children. He always intended to have his mistresses on the side.

Royal weddings then and now: Princess Diana, Kate Middleton, and Meghan Markle.

Dr. Dawson: I've heard or read the pro and cons of your marriage to Prince Charles. His father, Prince Philip, pushed him to propose and marry you because you fit the right profile. You were a virgin and noble by birth.

Princess Diana: Yes, flexible, and submissive is the key to understanding my attraction to the royal family. They expected to twist me like a pretzel into a regal robot. What else have you heard on the con side against me?

Dr. Dawson: The case against you is that you brought a lot of insecurities into your marriage with Prince Charles. You had a distressed childhood. Your father beat your mother, parents divorced, you lacked discipline and had school problems, mood swings, obsessive-compulsive behavior, and were a pathological liar. True?

Princess Diana: Charles sabotaged our marriage by being rude, insensitive, cold, indifferent, hard, mean, nasty, and harsh. My concerns were ignored. He snubbed my friends. How much could I take?

Is Meghan Markle or Kate Middleton more similar to Princess Diana? Princess Diana, who had a heart of gold, did charity work helping young and old who were sick or in need. Similarly, Meghan does charity work and has strong opinions. Kate is married to the future king and strictly follows royal protocol. Meghan can more easily bend royal rules, and she does at times. The press has pointed out Meghan's fashion quirks the Queen dislikes such as dark nail polish, mismatched earrings, dresses worn without pantyhose, and deliberately messy hair. Meghan has long been a feminist and an animal rights activist. So Meghan appears to be more of a rebel like Diana was.

Dr. Dawson: The people in Charles' camp have some objection to you. Want to hear their side?

Princess Diana: This is bloody ripping. I'd like a laugh. Tell me.

Dr. Dawson: You were gloomy and miserable from the onset of your marriage to Charles. You were not in love with Charles. You loved being Princess of Wales – you got off on the royal title and not Prince Charles. You made no effort to show any empathy for Charles.

Left: Lady Diana Frances Spencer, the Princess of Wales. Center: Diana, Charles. Right: Prince William and wife, Kate Middleton. Kate seems to be handling her royal duties successfully as Diana did.

Princess Diana: Amusing lies. What else?

Dr. Dawson: You were: 1) egotistical, narcissistic, self-centered, and obsessed with your desires; 2) you were demanding, stubborn, lying, cheating, and faithless; 3) you rejected some of his closest friends; 4) you disrespected his interests and hobbies.

Can you handle more insults? 1) You came across as sick because you came from a disturbed family full of marital and mental illness. 2) You have eating disorders, bulimia, self-destructive, cutting yourself, and suicidal threats.

Princess Diana: Oh, now I'm the ego-maniac? Suicidal? Let's hear more of my faults.

Dr. Dawson: A) Your approach to marriage was problematic. B) You created fictions about Charles and gossiped false stories about him. C) You were sneaking around with lovers and cheating on him. D) And to top it off, you wouldn't give him oral sex.

Pictured are Lady Diana Spencer and Camilla Parker-Bowles at Ludlow Races where Prince Charles was competing.

Princess Diana: Yes, if I'd just submit to kinky sex, marriage to Charles would be heaven. I will admit I rejected his closest friends, who were his lovers like Camilla. Well, Doctor, you've got your work cut out for you to cure me. I'm a tough nut to crack with all my defects.

1

Princess Diana was about to end her fairy-tale life at about 20 minutes after midnight on August 31st, 1997, in a car crash in the Alma Tunnel in Paris. Moments before, the Ritz Hotel security camera caught her in a down mood, frazzled and stressed-out as she headed for the Mercedes, the car in which she would end her life.

At the time of her death, she was with Dodi Fayed, 42, a kind of sketchy, trust-fund playboy. She'd known Dodi for only six weeks – the unfortunate couple had been on a cruise on a yacht off Sardinia and had met in Paris for a romantic weekend. Both Diana and Dodi were damaged. Similarly, both separated from their mothers at an early age, both suffered insecurities. Only Dodi was a cocaine addict.

Diana was on an out-of-control downward spiral through the six-week sex affair. She had experienced some trauma and had various symptoms including her parents' divorce and neglect, she felt unworthy, had a food disorder, was a binge eater, bulimic, and, at times, into self-mutilation.

Conspiracy theories swirled around the deaths of Princess Diana and Marilyn Monroe.

Diana also was driven by a series of tawdry sex affairs, some said she was a pathological liar, had a twisted and confused identity and unstable self-image, and plunged into erratic behaviors.

An eerie parallel to the 36-year-old Diana's personality disorder and death is revealed when she's compared to Marilyn Monroe, the movie superstar, blonde-bombshell, who also died at 36. Like Diana – the 1980s sex symbol, Marilyn, who was America's most iconic 1950s sex symbol, led a free spirit's self-damaging lifestyle.

Their mothers abandoned both Princess Diana and Marilyn Monroe at an early age, both were blondes, and both were superstars in their spheres. Diana and Marilyn were sexually promiscuous, at times, in their lives; both were involved with men who were at the top status of their nations - Monroe was romantically involved with President JFK and Princess Diana married Prince Charles of England.

Both Marilyn and Diana attempted suicide; both died at age 36, both had conspiracy theories clouding the truth about their deaths. And both Marilyn and Diana appeared to have Borderline Personality Disorder.

Monroe struggled, and was unable to find an identity all her own – she sought an identity by jumping into marriages, crazy romances, and sex affairs. In the early part of her film acting career, she traded sex for movie parts from film execs, producers, and directors. Her sexual promiscuity, shattered relationships, and broken marriages were self-destructive.

Marilyn ended up in a cycle of erratic mood swings, inappropriate anger, temper fits, depression, insomnia, drug and alcohol abuse, suicide attempts, and mysterious death by suicide, or was it murder?

Diana, the tragic, enigmatic fairy-tale princess, was revealed in books and interviews to have had a hidden psychological, mental disorder behind her glamorous public image. She was exposed to have led a tortured life: she'd struggled to find acceptance and her identity within the royal family she'd joined after marrying Prince Charles.

Her moods were fitful, unpredictable, and erratic. Diana's friendships were unreliable and inconsistent. At times, shockingly thin, her bulimia was showing.

Princess Diana and Dodi Fayed both died in a car crash.

Her sexual promiscuity caused scandals. As more of Diana's layers were researched, peeled back, and examined, she seemed to naturally have a royal's sense of entitlement and be self-indulgent.

People close to Diana said she was 1) unpredictable, 2) egocentric, 3) aggressive, 4) insecure, 5) manipulative, 6) paranoid, 7) possessive, 8) easily bored, 9) a victim of horrible mood swings and 10) a habitual liar. Diana was a snooper and an eavesdropper, so suspicious she opened other people's letters.

In summary, Diana's life was a) an adultery scandal, b) shattered by mental illness, c) betrayal, d) mistrust, and e) revenge. But to paparazzi and media people, when royalty goes wrong, it makes good copy.

Left to right: Robert F. Kennedy, Marilyn Monroe, and John F. Kennedy. Marilyn was sexually involved with RFK and JFK in the last year of her life.

What was the eerie, mysterious connection between Diana and Marilyn Monroe? Both Marilyn and Diana reached great heights. If they were both mentally sick, how did they do it?

The casting-couch sex with Hollywood power players only helped Marilyn get some small roles in early films. She struggled as a model, took serious-minded "method" acting classes, and fought it out for the better acting roles.

Marilyn worked very hard for her success and beat the odds – until she was locked-into a downward spiral of 1) 2) troubled film shoots, 3) broken marriages, 4) self-destructive romances, 5) depression, 6) mood swings, and 7) substance abuse – mood-altering drugs mixed with alcohol, 8) drug overdoses, 9) suicide attempts, and 10) death by suicide or murder.

Compare and contrast Diana's mental disorder symptoms with Marilyn's. Diana overcame tough odds to marry the future King of England – a man many women had tried and failed to wed.

Ironically, Diana's friend, Elton John, sang a version of his ode to Marilyn Monroe, "Candle in the Wind," with lyrics rewritten for Diana.

Both Marilyn Monroe and Diana suffered from what's known as Borderline Personality Disorder (BPD). BPD is somewhat elusive, sometimes undiagnosed. Because doctors sometimes don't see the overall forest for the trees – clinicians sometimes only spot the obvious problems such as impulsive and self-destructive behaviors (abuse of drugs and alcohol, binge eating, bulimia, self-mutilation, cutting, etc.).

Borderline Personality Disorder (BPD) characteristics include 1) a confused identity, 2) unstable self-image; 3) erratic mood swings; 4) extreme fear of rejection, and 5) intense fears of abandonment; 6) an inability to sustain relationships; 7) persistent feelings of loneliness, 8) boredom and chronic feelings of emptiness; 9) depression; and 10) impulsive and self-destructive behavior such as A) substance abuse of drugs and alcohol, B) eating disorders, and C) self-mutilation.

Diana experienced most of these BPD symptoms in her adult life in severe and chronic ways – according to her behavior, her admissions in interviews, and insights offered by her family and friends.

According to the Diagnostic & Statistical Manual of the American Psychiatric Association, for BPD to be diagnosed, at least five of the following signs and symptoms must be present. Diana, like Marilyn Monroe, seemed to show most of these signs and symptoms: 1) intense fears of abandonment; 2) a pattern of unstable relationships; 3) unstable self-image; 4) impulsive, and 5) self-destructive behaviors; 6) suicidal behavior or self-injury; 7) wide mood swings; 8) chronic feelings of emptiness; 9) inappropriate anger; 10) periods of paranoia, and 11) loss of contact with reality.

She was born July 1st, 1961, Diana Frances Spencer at Park House in Norfolk, England. Her parents were Edward John Spencer, known as "Johnnie," and Frances Roche. Diana was not a princess when she was born. But she was from one of Great Britain's oldest and most influential families.

The Spencer family was allied to the Royal family for more than five hundred years. Her father, "Johnnie," had the title of Viscount Althorp and served as the Queen Mother's equerry. Diana's mother's parents were Lord and Lady Maurice and Ruth Fermoy.

In 1969, Diana's parents were divorced. In 1975, Diana's father became the eighth Earl of Spencer, and she became Lady Diana. At age 16, Diana first met Prince Charles at Althorp. She had been attending a finishing school in Switzerland in 1978, she dropped out and returned to London to find work as a kindergarten teacher in 1979.

Diana began dating Prince Charles in July 1980. July 29th, 1981, the wedding of Prince Charles to Lady Diana took place. Prince William was born on June 21st, 1982. On September 15th, 1984, Prince Harry was born.

By 1986, Prince Charles resumed his romance with Camilla Parker Bowles. Diana complained, "There were three of us in this marriage…" Diana began her first out-of-marriage sexual affair with Captain James Hewitt. In 1989, Diana's conversation with James Gilbey was recorded on December 31st – it was later released and caused a scandal.

In December 1992, Princess Diana and Prince Charles formally separated. After some tell-all books and interviews with Diana, the divorce of Prince Charles and the Princess of Wales was finalized on August 28th, 1996. After her death on August 31st, 1997, her funeral was held on September 6th, and she was honored as a member of the royal family.

The most critical incident, early in Diana's life, was the divorce of her parents. As Princess Diana later recalled: "The biggest disruption was when Mummy decided to leg it. That's the vivid memory we have – the four of us. For my brother and me, it was a very wishy-washy and painful experience… We had so many changes of nannies… My brother and I, if we didn't like them, we used to stick pins in their chairs and throw their clothes out the window."

"We always thought they were a threat because they tried to take my mother's position. I always felt very different from everyone else, very detached... The divorce helped me to relate to anyone else who is upset in their family life, whether it be step-father syndrome or mother or whatever. I understand it. Been there, done it..."

Diana recalled romantic stirrings as an adolescent: "I had crushes, severe crushes on all sorts of people, especially my sister's boyfriends. If they ever got chucked out from that department, I used to try my way. Anyway, that was a dead miss..."

Later, in London, as a bachelor girl, Diana said, "It was nice being in a flat with the girls. I loved that – it was great..." When news of Diana's sex scandals and BPD type issues was released, she complained: "I think I was so fed up with being seen as someone who was a basket case because I am a powerful person and I know that causes complications in the system that I live in..."

The Queen and her husband, Philip, tried an informal family-therapy session with Diana and Charles. Philip asked, "Can you tell us what's the matter, Diana?" His daughter-in-law collapsed in tears. She kept sobbing and refused offers of comfort. "Well, Charles," the Queen desperately asked her son, "Can you explain to us?" "What?" replied Prince Charles. "And read it all in the newspapers tomorrow? No, thank you." That ended the first and last royal family-therapy session.

In summary, I've indicated that there is evidence that Princess Diana suffered from Borderline Personality Disorder. Diana showed signs and symptoms of BPD such as 1) a confused identity and a twisted self-image; 2) sharp and wide mood swings; 3) depression; 4) extreme fear of rejection and intense fears of abandonment; 5) an inability to sustain relationships; 6) a pattern of unstable relationships; 7) suicidal behavior or self-injury; 8) unstable self-image; 9) persistent feelings of loneliness; 10) boredom and chronic feelings of emptiness; 11) inappropriate anger, 12) temper tantrums; 13) periods of paranoia; 14) loss of contact with reality, 15) and delusions of persecution.

Diana confirmed her BPD signs and symptoms herself in interviews or in what she revealed to others, by her behavior and from insights coming from her family or friends. She revealed her various BPD characteristics in her psychotherapy sessions.

2

Princess Diana revealed that Charles was considering her as a possible wife when she was 16 in this chapter. It was in the tradition of the monarchy for the prince to marry a young virgin of noble birth. Queen Elizabeth had met Prince Philip when she was 13.

Charles had gone through a process of affairs with various young women and eliminated many girls from his list for a possibly suitable wife. His choice, who would become Princess of Wales, needed to meet some qualifications – a virgin; born into aristocratic, noble, royal circles; and in the correct religion (Protestant, Anglican, Church of England).

Teenage Lady Diana Spencer was on a ski holiday in Val Claret. Young teenage Diana (right).

The more feminist, experienced young women with a past sex life were acceptable for a one-night stand or a quickie affair. Royal men of the English monarchy preferred an upper-class teenage virgin who was submissive and flexible. We follow Diana from first meeting Charles in this chapter until he proposes to her, and she accepts.

Dr. Dawson: Okay, Diana, can you go back to you at age 16? How did you meet Charles, and what happened?

Young teenage Diana.

Princess Diana: Charles came to stay at Althorp in Northhampton, where we'd moved to when I was 13. I was 16 and he was seeing my sister Sarah. Charles was sad, my sister was crazy about him, and I felt unattractive at the time.

Dr. Dawson: What was wrong with your looks?

Princess Diana: I was overweight, kind of chubby, and wore no make-up. But for some reason, there was some chemistry, and I was bubbly, extroverted, and funny at dinner. Charles got a kick out of me, he asked me to dance after dinner, and he asked me to show him the gallery.

Teenage Diana. Diana, with her sister Lady Sarah McCorquodale watching tennis at Wimbledon.

Dr. Dawson: Was that a step in the romantic direction?

Princess Diana: Yes. At that point, my sister Sarah rushed up and told me to fuck off. The next day he was coming up to me and showing me a lot of attention, which shocked me and pissed-off my sister, Sarah.

Dr. Dawson: But you were only 16, is that correct?

Princess Diana: From then I only saw him once in a while for the next two years when he was seeing my sister Sarah. Sarah was bloody thrilled to be seeing him.

Lady Sarah, Diana's sister, and Diana as a teenager.

Dr. Dawson: When did he invite you out?

Princess Diana: Then Charles turned 30, and he threw a dance party to celebrate. He invited Sarah and me also. Sarah was surprised that I was invited to Buckingham Palace along with her. She kept asking me why I was invited.

Dr. Dawson: How did your sister take it?

Left to right: Lucia Santa Cruz, Prince Charles, Jane Ward, Prince Charles. Lucia and Charles are leaving the Fortune Theater. Jane Ward was a girlfriend of Prince Charles. "The Firm," the royal family, screened-out females who were not marriage material.

Princess Diana: Charles again showed me some interest that annoyed my sister.

Dr. Dawson: Was there some romantic intrigue in the subtext of this invitation?

Princess Diana: At the time, I was naïve and clueless about what Charles was planning. I found out years later that Charles was being pressured by Prince Philip and perhaps some others in the monarchy to find a suitable wife.

Prince Charles with Lady Sarah Spencer in 1977. Unfortunately, Lady Sarah, like Diana, also battled an eating disorder. Royal fan: Farrah greeted Prince Charles during his 1977 trip to the U.S.

But, now being 30, time was running out for Charles to get married to an appropriate virgin from the noble class.

Dr. Dawson: Why was the selection process so tricky for Charles?

Princess Diana: Royal men and their families scrutinized girls. The girl would need to be of the correct religion – Protestant, Anglican in the Church of England.

Caroline Longman, former girlfriend of Prince Charles in 1979 (left). Lady Jane Wellesley (right) and Prince Charles. Both were his former girlfriends pre-Diana.

Some of his lovers were of the wrong religion, and Catholics, Buddhists, or whatever were out.

Dr. Dawson: What other criteria?

Princess Diana: Girls who were not virgins were out. I was still a virgin because I had run-off boyfriends as too much trouble. I was emotionally crazed and couldn't handle a big romance in my teens.

Lord Mountbatten (left) coached and mentored Prince Charles on his love affairs and girlfriends. Queen Mother (right) and Prince Charles at the 1979 funeral of Lord Mountbatten, held at Westminster Abbey. Diana noticed how sad Charles was at the funeral.

Dr. Dawson: Well, it might seem to most that every eligible young lady in the U.K. would love to marry Prince Charles. What was reality?

Princess Diana: Several young ladies who were smarter than I declined when he proposed marriage to them. They both saw through Charles and realized that the Princess of Wales title and marriage to my husband would be the end of their freedom.

Pictured is Anna Oates Wallace (b. November 19, 1955), daughter of wealthy Scottish landowner Hamish Wallace. She was Charles' final fling before Diana.

Dr. Dawson: Any other negatives?

Princess Diana: Joining the monarchy as a princess would mean attending tedious rituals, stuffy charity events, and endless social functions requiring the proper Princess of Wales' behavior, and incredible press scrutiny and harassment.

Dr. Dawson: What was the next step in Charles checking you out?

An Australian beauty kissed Prince Charles in Perth in 1979.

Princess Diana: In July 1980, I was invited to Petworth by Philip de Pass to stay over two nights. Philip said Charles was staying over. He was casual about the invitation. Philip said a young lady like myself might entertain the Prince of Wales.

Dr. Dawson: What happened at Petworth?

Princess Diana: I sat next to Philip and was socializing when Charles arrived. Again it was bizarre to me at the time. Charles was all over me like a bad rash. It was flattering to me as a teenage girl. But it was peculiar to me that he was so unmistakable in flirting with me.

Prince Charles and Camilla, Duchess of Cornwall, laughing. Diana suspected them of laughing at her after she married Prince Charles. Right: Prince Charles and Princess Diana on their honeymoon.

Dr. Dawson: What was his next move?

Princess Diana: We went to a barbeque that night. He sat next to me on a bale of hay. I spoke to him about seeing him at the funeral for Lord Mountbatten. I told him he looked so sad when he walked up the aisle.

And I said my heart went out to him in his grief. I told him he seemed so lonely and he should have somebody to look after him. I'd heard he just broke up with Anna Wallace.

Prince Charles and Camilla (blonde woman). The courtship of Lady Di and Prince Charles (right).

Dr. Dawson: What happened with Anna Wallace?

Princess Diana: Anna was the daughter of wealthy Scots landowners. The gossip was that Charles fell hard for her. The problem was that she was just too much of a feminist.

Dr. Dawson: Too feminist? How so?

Prince Charles and Princess Diana on their honeymoon on board Britannia. Lady Sarah and Prince Charles in 1977.

Princess Diana: Anna was sexy but assertive. She was one of those very independent and unrestrained, spontaneous and uninhibited women who kind of represented the change in sexual politics we were discussing. She was not overwhelmed in having the Prince of Wales courting her.

Dr. Dawson: How did it end with Anna?

Princess Diana: It's funny. Or it was funny then. Charles took Anna to Balmoral, and while he was making love to her on the beach, he spotted the press watching them with binoculars. He jumped up and ran into the bushes to hide. He left her alone. She was shocked at being mistreated and left alone.

Diana with Sir Robert Fellowes. Lord Robert Fellowes and his wife Jane (Diana's sister).

Dr. Dawson: That was the end of it?

Princess Diana: At later social functions – a birthday ball for Queen Elizabeth and then a polo ball – Charles ignored Anna and instead got intoxicated with Camilla. Camilla was always checking out Charles' young women.

Dr. Dawson: What was the significance?

Pictured are The Queen with the Duke of Edinburgh, Andrew, Edward, Anne, and Charles, in front of Balmoral Castle during their annual summer holiday in August 1972. Charles dated Sabrina Guinness in 1979 (right).

Princess Diana: I laughed at the conflict he had with Anna and their breakup. What I didn't realize at the time was that it was a cautionary tale for me.

Eventually, it would be my turn to be beaten-up emotionally and abused by Charles with him and Camilla laughing at me over drinks behind the scenes.

Dr. Dawson: Okay, let's get back to that hay bale and the barbeque. You showed Charles some empathy because he was sad at Lord Mountbatten's funeral and...?

In 1980, Diana visited the royal family at Balmoral Castle in Scotland to see her sister, Lady Jane, who married Robert Fellowes, the queen's assistant.

Princess Diana: The moment after I showed him some sympathy, he almost jumped all over me. He had his arm around me suddenly and was squeezing me. I was perplexed and astonished.

We went on talking the evening away. I was afraid Charles was going to kiss me, so I just kept talking and talking as a way of dissuading him.

Dr. Dawson: Did it work?

Ladi Di during the courtship. Prince Charles and Princess Diana during their honeymoon.

Princess Diana: I think he was frustrated. But by the end of the night, he invited me to come to London and accompany him at Buckingham Palace the next day. I felt I was being yanked about, and I politely turned him down. I was supposed to be staying at Philip's place.

Dr. Dawson: What happened next with Charles?

Princess Diana: He invited me to Cowes on the *Britannia*. When I got aboard, a lot of his older friends were there. I was alarmed and anxious at that yacht party because there was some social subtext I was not aware of.

Diana Spencer is receiving a kiss from a friend at a polo match before her marriage. Princess Diana and Prince Charles married.

Charles or somebody was talking about me because many of his friends were all over me like I was his big social secret.

Dr. Dawson: What was the next meeting with Charles?

Princess Diana: Apparently, this was all some pre-courtship dance. My sister Jane's husband, Robert Fellowes, was private secretary to the Queen.

I went to stay with my sister Jane at Balmoral. Balmoral made me nervous. The procedures were a mystery to me.

Dr. Dawson: Was it horrible once you got there?

Pictured is Diana at a polo match in 1981 during her engagement to Prince Charles. Prince Charles crossed his arms, leaving Diana to hug him. Was Charles defensive?

Princess Diana: It all worked out. I was assigned a room and a single bed. I brought in a few pieces of luggage. The press had gotten tipped that I was at Balmoral.

So I stayed hidden at the castle. Camilla and her husband were there. In retrospect, I wonder if she were there to check me out. Probably.

Dr. Dawson: What did you do with Charles at Balmoral Castle?

Pictured are Charles Earl Spencer, Diana's brother, Princess Diana, and Prince Charles in 1985.

Princess Diana: He invited me to go for walks. I went to a barbeque with him. I was very excited and thought it was magnificent. I was so completely naïve.

Dr. Dawson: What was the next stage of the romance with Prince Charles?

Princess Diana: Well, I'd taken a flat with three other single girls in London. An employment agency sent me out on jobs, I had nanny jobs, took a cooking course, and gained some weight. My bachelor girl's life was fun, but the press interfered with my love life.

Lady Diana Spencer and her flatmate Carolyn Pride (left). On February 23, 1981, the night before her engagement to Prince Charles was officially announced, Diana left her flat and moved into Clarence House.

Dr. Dawson: What was the scene like?

Princess Diana: Fortunately, my three flatmates were loyal and were great with me against the press. I'd heard later that Queen Elizabeth was exasperated by Charles, who was pressured to hurry up and marry a proper young lady.

Finally, Charles rang me and said he had something to ask me. I expected a proposal the next time we met. I asked my flatmates what I should do or say.

Windsor Castle is a royal residence at Windsor in the English county of Berkshire. It is strongly associated with the English and succeeding British royal family, and embodies almost 1000 years of architectural history.

Dr. Dawson: Where did you meet with Charles?

Princess Diana: I arrived the next day in the early evening at Windsor. Now keep in mind that I'd never had a boyfriend and so I was innocent and guileless about the romance between a man and a woman.

Dr. Dawson: How did Charles come across to you?

Prince Charles, Princess Diana, Prince Harry, and Meghan Markle.

Princess Diana: Charles sat with me and started saying these squidgy, gooey, and sentimental things like, "Darling, I've missed you very much…" Now he had not even kissed me. Suddenly out of the blue, he blurted out, "Will you marry me?"

Dr. Dawson: What was your reaction?

Princess Diana: I thought he was joking because it was so shocking and not based on any developing love. I just giggled and said, "Yeah, okay…"

Diana received an awkward and unromantic proposal from Charles.

Dr. Dawson: What did Charles say next?

Princess Diana: He was serious and went on about how I should realize that someday I would be Queen. I didn't think I would be Queen. But I went along with him and said, "Okay. I love you so much!"

Dr. Dawson: Did he follow-up with any other comments?

Princess Diana, Prince Charles, and Camilla Parker Bowles. Diana's engagement and marriage were haunted by Charles's love and obsession with Camilla.

Princess Diana: Then he replied with a strange remark, "Whatever love means." Again, I was so naïve that I didn't realize he didn't love me, and I was just a pawn in the monarchy game to move the Firm down the road.

He faked a love-struck, infatuated look for my benefit. Charles then ran upstairs and rang up his mother to give the Queen the news.

Dr. Dawson: How did your family and friends take the news of your engagement to Prince Charles?

Left: Lady Diana and her flatmate Carolyn Pride. Right: Charles, Diana, William, and Kate.

Princess Diana: My girls back at the flat were ecstatic when I told them he proposed and I said yes. We went out and drove around town quite happily. Now I realize I was very immature and getting myself into romantic trouble.

The romance was all on my side since Charles never loved me. Daddy and Mummy were happy when I called them the next morning with the news. I then called my brother and told him I was engaged.

"Who you engaged to, sis?" he asked.

"Prince Charles," I told him.

"No, seriously," he said. "Who are you engaged to?"

3

Diana's childhood critical incidents, such as her parents' divorce, were so traumatic that they may have triggered a complex Borderline Personality Disorder (BPD) syndrome. She had nasty signs and symptoms which would become a partly untreated cancer eating away at her psyche until she died at age 36?

I checked a series of sources and researched Diana's childhood into her teenage years. Some sources, well-meant, seemed a bit sugar-coated. Other sources were not afraid to get into the dirt, serve up some racy bits of her parents' romantic or sex life, and the downside of parenting.

Diana's childhood and teen years have been perceived in light of her troubles and remarkable life as an adult. So, for example, when Diana's bulimia, suicidal, or self-mutilation behavior was analyzed, her parents' divorce and her mother's leaving was exaggerated as significant trauma.

Left: Diana's stepmother, father. Right: Raine, Diana's "wicked" stepmother, Princess Diana. Diana had a complicated relationship with her stepmother.

Diana grew up in Park House, situated on the Sandringham estate. Diana's relationship with her stepmother was particularly bad. She resented Raine, whom she called a "bully," and on one occasion Diana "pushed her down the stairs." She later described her childhood as "very unhappy" and "very unstable, the whole thing."

The Princess Diana literature reported that Diana's family was a typical, sheltered, privileged, affluent family living in a mansion. Approximately fifty percent of marriages in Western, developed countries end in divorce - so Diana's parents' divorce is a standard variable and not a significant automatic trauma. I'd suspect that Diana has a genetic predisposition to break down with Borderline Personality Disorder when combined with environmental factors.

Left: Diana's stepfather, Peter Shand Kydd, Diana's mother. Right: Frances, Diana's mother, Princess Diana.

On the Norfolk estate of the Viscount Althorp (later the eighth Earl Spencer) and his wife, Diana, and her two older sisters - joined in 1964 by a brother, Charles – they were surrounded by servants, including a butler and the governess.

The children ate their meals with a nanny in a house that was a kind of annex to Sandringham, the royal family's country place near the North Sea. It was, Charles recalled, an "upbringing out of a different age, a distant way of living from your parents."

When Diana was 6, that distance grew greater and more difficult to overcome. Her parents separated: her mother had fallen in love with Peter Shand Kydd, a wallpaper tycoon, and was named as correspondent in his divorce. The viscount and viscountess soon divorced in a most ungenteel manner that the tabloids devoured.

Princess Diana – childhood photos.

Both had numerous links to the royal family. Diana's maternal grandmother was a Woman of the Bedchamber and a close friend of the Queen Mother. In the Royal Household of the United Kingdom, the term Woman of the Bedchamber is used to describe a woman (usually a daughter of a peer) attending either a queen regnant or queen consort, in the role of Lady-in-Waiting.

Her father had served as Equerry to both George VI and Elizabeth II, who was godmother to Diana's brother. In contemporary use, an equerry is a personal attendant, usually upon a sovereign, a member of a royal family, or a national representative.

After a nasty custody battle, the children began shuttling between their parents' houses. Diana could not bear to take sides. When each parent gave her a new dress to wear to a cousin's wedding, she was all but paralyzed. "I can't remember," she said later, "which one I wore, but I remember being traumatized by it because it would show favoritism."

Princess Diana and her mother.

Despite their creature comforts, which included a swimming pool and a tennis court, Diana and her siblings were anything but comfortable. "The whole thing was precarious," Diana recalled. "I remember my mother crying. Daddy never spoke to us about it. We could never ask questions. Too many nannies."

The Spencer children went through a string of nannies. One woman disciplined Diana and her brother by whacking their heads together, and another secretly laced drinks with laxatives if the girls misbehaved.

Diana at her London flat.

Controlling spoiled children can be difficult, and I don't know if these horror stories about Diana's childhood issues are accurate or significant. However, it is all relative - so luxury problems for poor kids could cause anxiety for upper-class children like Diana. A rough childhood involving divorce could add to Diana's fear of divorcing Prince Charles.

Like many upper-class Britons, at the age of nine, Diana was sent to boarding school. She was high-spirited, grew tall, and athletic. Diana, compassionate, volunteered at a mental hospital. Her kindhearted nature helped offset her dim academic record. As an adult, she casually referred to herself as "thick as a plank."

Left: Diana and her brother, Charles Earl Spencer. Right: Park House, Sandringham Estate.

At 16, she failed all her O-Levels, standardized tests for British students. The O-Levels, or Ordinary Levels, typically represent a total of 11 years of study and mark the end of the secondary-education cycle. After that, she left school in England and spent a semester at a Swiss finishing school, where she improved her skiing and her French.

In 1979 her parents set her up in a London flat, which she shared with three other young women in the fashionable Sloane Square area. Lady Diana worked as a part-time nanny, a house cleaner, and a part-time kindergarten staffer - the last job she had before signing on as Princess of Wales.

Young Lady Diana, in her late teens.

She had a moneyed background, but at 18, she was a young girl who enjoyed playing pranks and had a sense of fun. Prince Charles was 12 years older than Diana.

Diana was baptized at St. Mary Magdalene Church, Sandringham. Diana had three siblings: Sarah, Jane, and Charles. Diana also had an infant brother, John, who died only a year before she was born. The desire for an heir added strain to the Spencers' marriage, and Lady Althorp was reportedly sent to Harley Street clinics in London to determine the cause of the problem.

The experience was described as humiliating by Diana's younger brother, Charles: "It was a dreadful time for my parents and probably the root of their divorce because I don't think they ever got over it." Diana grew up in Park House, which was situated near to the Sandringham estate.

Diana and her brother at Park House, Sandringham.

The root of Diana's insecurity lay in her upbringing, despite its privileges. Her family was living on the Queen's estate at Sandringham, where her father had rented Park House. He had special connections because he had been a royal equerry for both King George VI and the young Queen Elizabeth II.

But Diana was only six when her parents split up; she would always remember her mother's departing - the children became pawns in a bitter custody dispute. Lady Diana was sent to boarding school, eventually attending West Heath Public School in Kent. There she excelled at sport, particularly swimming. In later years, she warmly recalled school-day memories and supported her old school.

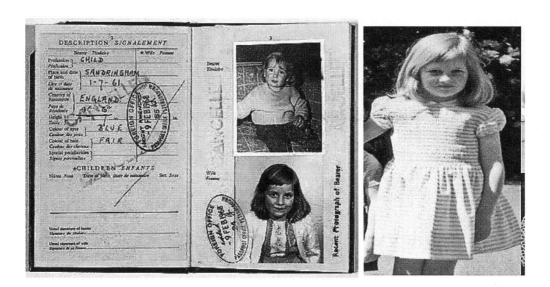

Diana's passport. Diana as a young girl.

Diana was eight years old when her parents divorced after her mother had an affair with Peter Shand Kydd. Diana remembered Lord Althorp loading suitcases in the car and Lady Althorp driving away through the gates of Park House. Diana lived with her mother in London during her parents' separation.

Shortly afterward, Lord Althorp eventually won custody of Diana with support from his former mother-in-law, Ruth Roche, Baroness Fermoy. Diana went to school at Riddlesworth Hall near Diss, Norfolk, and later attended boarding school at The New School at West Heath, in Sevenoaks, Kent. In 1973, Lord Althorp began a relationship with Raine, Countess of Dartmouth, the only daughter of Alexander McCorquodale and Barbara Cartland.

One nanny, Janet Thompson, who took care of Diana for four years, said Diana was not an unmanageable child but could be obstinate: "Simply obstinate. She would not cooperate. I think she may have seen how her elder sister, Sarah, was behaving and copied her."

Diana, Sarah, her sister, and Diana. Sarah set some bad examples for Diana in her childhood.

Sarah was the last one able to offer guidance to Diana. Her behavior was out of control, but funny. She once rode her horse into the living room at Park House to bother her grandmother, Lady Fermoy. She was kicked out of boarding school for getting intoxicated. Sarah suffered from the eating disorder Anorexia Nervosa in her early twenties. Anorexia Nervosa is an emotional disorder characterized by an obsessive desire to lose weight by refusing to eat.

Diana became known as Lady Diana when her father inherited the title of Earl Spencer on June 9th, 1975. Lady Dartmouth, unpopular with Diana, married Lord Spencer at Caxton Hall, London, on July 14th, 1976. Diana was often noted for her shyness while growing up, but she did take an interest in both music and dancing. She also had a great interest in children.

Left: Diana at the Institut Alpin Videmanette, a finishing school in Rougemont, Switzerland. Center: Diana. Right: Riddlesworth Hall, an all-girls boarding school.

In 1968, Diana was sent to Riddlesworth Hall, an all-girls boarding school. While she was young, she attended a local public school. She did not shine academically and was moved to West Heath Girls' School (later reorganized as The New School at West Heath) in Sevenoaks, Kent, where she was regarded as a poor student, having attempted and failed all of her O-Levels twice. The O-Levels, in the UK except for Scotland, are the lower of the two main levels of standardized examinations in secondary schools.

However, she showed a particular talent for music as an accomplished pianist. Her outstanding community spirit was recognized with an award from West Heath. In 1977, she left West Heath and briefly attended Institut Alpin Videmanette, a finishing school in Rougemont, Switzerland.

Lady Diana, age 16. Prince Charles and Lady Sarah Spencer circa the time Charles first met Diana when she was 16.

After attending finishing school at the Institut Alpin Videmanette in Switzerland, she moved to London. She began working with children, eventually becoming a nursery assistant at the Young England School. Diana had played with Prince Andrew and Prince Edward as a child while her family rented Park House, a property owned by Queen Elizabeth II and situated on the Sandringham Estate.

At age 16, she first met her future husband, who was then in a relationship with her older sister, Sarah. Diana also excelled in swimming and diving and longed to be a professional ballerina with the Royal Ballet. She studied ballet for a time, but then grew too tall for the profession.

Left: Lady Diana at the Swiss finishing school, 1978. Right: Diana while she was living in her mother's apartment, 1978.

Diana moved to London in 1978 and lived in her mother's apartment, as her mother then spent most of the year in Scotland. Soon afterward, a residence was purchased as an 18th birthday present, at Coleherne Court in Earls Court. She lived there until 1981 with three roommates.

In London, she took an advanced cooking course at her mother's suggestion, although she never became a great cook, and worked as a dance instructor for youth, until a skiing accident caused her to miss three months of work. She then found employment as a playgroup pre-school assistant, did some cleaning work for her sister Sarah and several of her friends, and worked as a hostess at parties. Diana also spent time working as a nanny for an American family living in London.

4

Princess Diana's engagement and marriage to Prince Charles is discussed in this chapter. She was torn between her fantasies that she was in love with Charles versus the reality that he was in love with Camilla. His behavior showed that even in the crucial time of her engagement and marriage, he was more concerned with Camilla.

She admitted some BPD symptoms in this chapter such as her eating disorder, Bulimia Nervosa – an emotional disorder involving distortion of body image and an obsessive desire to lose weight, in which bouts of extreme overeating are followed by depression and self-induced vomiting, purging, or fasting. She experienced shocking mood swings and depression. Loneliness and abandonment fears were frequent.

Dr. Dawson: What was your next move after getting engaged to marry Charles?

Princess Diana: I flew down to Australia to get some help from Mummy about the wedding to Charles.

Baby Diana, being held by her mother, Frances, at her baptism. **Princess Diana and her mother, Frances Shand Kydd.**

Dr. Dawson: Frances Shand Kydd. What did she feel about you marrying Charles? Was she thrilled because you'd be the Princess of Wales, possibly the future Queen?

Princess Diana: Mummy was against it. I argued with her. I told her I loved Charles.

Dr. Dawson: Why was she against you marrying Prince Charles?

Pictured are Princess Diana and her grandmother, Lady Fermoy.   On July 22nd, 1983, Diana was greeted by her maternal grandmother, Lady Ruth Fermoy, at St Nicholas' Chapel, King's Lynn, Norfolk (right).

Princess Diana: Mummy compared marrying Charles to her marrying Daddy. She said she was too young to marry Johnnie Spencer – her first marriage. It was too rushed. Mummy and Daddy were incompatible. And Charles and I are mismatched. I should have listened to her.

Dr. Dawson: Did Frances have any other objections?

Pictured are Edward John Spencer, 8th Earl Spencer (1924-1992), and the Honorable Frances Burke Roche (1936-2005). Diana's mother was 12 years younger than her first husband. Princess Diana and Prince Charles (right) were all smiles after their engagement announcement in 1981.

Princess Diana: She emphasized our age differences and that I'd be overwhelmed with the responsibilities and duties of being Princess Diana. Mummy warned me that her mother, Lady Fermoy, my grandmother, was scheming behind the scenes to get Charles to marry me. I should have picked up on the clue that Charles didn't love me when I was in Australia. He didn't bother to ring me up.

The photo showed Princess Diana's engagement ring, which was an enormous sapphire surrounded by diamonds. The cost was 28,000 pounds or about $44,000 in U.S. dollars today. Prince Charles' wife, Diana, and mistress, Camilla.

Dr. Dawson: Did you call him?

Princess Diana: When I called him, he was always out and did not return my calls. It was all evidence that I was just an insignificant cog in the big wheel of the monarchy. I tried to make up excuses for Charles that he must be busy. The Firm – the senior royals of the Windsor family – couldn't have cared less about me.

Dr. Dawson: What happened when you returned from Australia?

Paparazzi's picture shows the newly engaged Lady Diana Frances Spencer, the youngest daughter of Edward John Spencer (left). Lady Diana (right) visited Broadlands to open a memorial to Lord Louis Mountbatten.

Princess Diana: When I got back from Australia, someone from Charles' office dropped off some flowers with no note. Charles did not even send them. The monarchy was just managing their Princess-of-Wales candidate.

Dr. Dawson: What was next?

Princess Diana: The engagement leading up to the wedding was insane. The press was harassing me with 30 to 40 paparazzi, reporters, and photographers all over me.

Princess Diana's and Kate Middleton's engagement rings.

They surrounded my flat while I was working as a kindergarten teacher. They followed my every move. They spied on me from a flat across the street. The papers would call me at 3 AM and asked me to confirm a story they were about to publish.

Dr. Dawson: Did the press follow you when you traveled?

Princess Diana: When I drove my car, I tried to lose the press by pulling through intersections when the light turned red. But with 30 to 40 from the media after me, it was almost hopeless.

Bolehyde Manor (left) was owned by the Duchess of Cornwall when she was Camilla Parker Bowles. It was a retreat where Prince Charles and Camilla made love. Prince Charles and Camilla Parker Bowles were spoofed on Saturday Night Live (right).

One night I was meeting Charles, so I climbed out the kitchen window to escape the press. It overlooked a side street, and I snuck away. I got no support from Charles, and the Palace press office told me I was on my own.

Dr. Dawson: You got no support from Charles?

Princess Diana: Zero support from Charles. He was always moaning about how hard our engagement was on Camilla! If I wasn't so naïve and immature, I would have called off the wedding.

Princess Diana and Prince Charles on the grounds of Buckingham Palace in February 1981, just days after they announced their engagement. Princess Diana and the paparazzi (right).

Dr. Dawson: What was his focus?

Princess Diana: Charles complained that Camilla was whining, cranky, and squealing about the press at Bolehyde. I had stayed with the Parker-Bowles before I got engaged.

Camilla was telling me not to push Charles into anything. It was all so vague to me then. But Charles was telling Camilla everything behind my back.

Diana's gemstone choker is now part of a Special Exhibit, "Dress for the Occasion" showing dresses worn by QEII, and jewels from QEII's collection. Buckingham Palace.

Dr. Dawson: Why was Camilla upset?

Princess Diana: She had 2 or 3 reporters and photographers at Bolehyde. Charles rang me up and complained that Camilla had lots of press harassing her – 2 or 3 reporters. I didn't complain to Charles, but I always had 30 to 40 paps and reporters in front of my place or chasing me.

Dr. Dawson: What happened next?

Camilla and Diana at Ludlow racecourse to watch Charles competing. Romantic history: Charles and Camilla leaving a theatre together in 1975. They rekindled and continued their love affair.

Princess Diana: I moved to the Queen's residence in London – Clarence House. I walked in, and nobody bothered to welcome me. They asked me why I was there. I said I was told to move to Clarence House, and a police officer was assigned to me.

Dr. Dawson: Why was that?

An enthusiastic fox hunter, Prince Charles (left), was at the New Forest Hunt in 1999. Charles' girlfriend Camilla was a keen huntswoman (right).

Princess Diana: My engagement was about to be officially announced. The policeman told me that, after the announcement, my freedom would be over.

I naively thought it was funny. But then I was trapped without knowing it. My engagement was in all the papers. From there, I moved into Buckingham Palace.

Dr. Dawson: What was up at the Palace?

Princess Diana: Suddenly Kings and Queens and Presidents were stopping by to give me wedding presents. The atmosphere at the Palace towards me was icy.

Lady Diana and Prince Charles Tea Towel (left). A Royal Wedding of Prince Charles and Lady Diana souvenir scarf (right).

My grandma Ruth, Lady Fermoy, warned me that the royals' sense of humor and lifestyle would not appeal to me. She was right.

Dr. Dawson: What was so bad at the Palace?

Princess Diana: There was so much trickery, deception, and falseness. To add to the circus, Charles was always busy sending flowers, presents, and little love notes to Camilla, which I'd catch now and then. His alibi was that she was a sick friend.

Dr. Dawson: How did you feel about Camilla and Charles when you were about to marry Charles?

Princess Diana: I overheard Charles chatting sentimentally with Camilla on the phone. He told her he'd always love her despite marrying me out of duty.

Diana and Charles (left) during their honeymoon entertained aboard ship Mr. & Mrs. Anwar Sadat. Jealousy over Camilla drove fights Diana had with Charles, who appeared unhappy in the photo (right).

We'd fight over Camilla and his attention to her. I was jealous and then depressed, how I hated that woman!

Dr. Dawson: Yet the press reported the two of you were seen together.

Princess Diana: She invited me to lunch during my engagement period. We had lunch. Her concern was about my activity when I was to live at Highgrove.

She asked me if I was going hunting on horseback. I didn't get why she was asking. I guessed she was planning on fox hunting with Charles and didn't want me in the way.

Pictured is Prince Charles, who purchased Highgrove House in 1980, with Princess Diana and their two boys.

Dr. Dawson: What else did Charles do with Camilla?

Princess Diana: About two weeks before we got married, Charles sent Camilla a bracelet symbolizing their love. I found the package, unwrapped it, and confronted Charles about sending the bracelet to Camilla.

We fought about it; he was moody with me. Charles cut me off. He was cold one moment and angry another.

Dr. Dawson: Why didn't you dump Charles?

Clarence House was the official residence of the Prince of Wales. August 4th, 1990: Princess Diana and the Royal family at Clarence House. The south front of Clarence House (right).

Princess Diana: When I told my sisters about this betrayal on Charles' part, they shrugged and said it was too late. At that point, the wedding was big business for the monarchy and England.

My sisters made a joke of it and said I could not chicken out because my face was on the towels they were selling to tourists. I was hoping he'd get Camilla out of his system. No such luck.

Pictured is Princess Diana's first curtsy to the Queen as the Princess Of Wales during the wedding ceremony at St Paul's Cathedral.

Dr. Dawson: Was Camilla an ongoing problem?

Princess Diana: On our honeymoon, I caught Charles wearing cufflinks engraved from Camilla while we had a white-tie dinner for President Sadat of Egypt. By that point, the jealousy was driving fights we'd have.

Dr. Dawson: Did Charles help with the wedding planning?

Pictured are Prince Charles and Princess Diana were on the balcony of Buckingham Palace on their wedding day.

Princess Diana: No. Before the wedding, Charles went on a tour of Australia and New Zealand. I was left to plan the wedding alone. It broke my heart when I'd catch him talking to Camilla on the phone.

He bought Highgrove House in the Duchy of Cornwall, which was only 11 miles from Camilla's house. He asked me to decorate the home.

Dr. Dawson: What was Charles' input on the wedding?

Princess Diana: He said he wanted the wedding at St. Paul's and not at Westminster Abbey because people could see better. He said the acoustics were superior at St. Paul's.

On their honeymoon, Princess Diana and Prince Charles embarked on an eleven-day Mediterranean cruise on the royal yacht Britannia (right), visiting Tunisia, Sardinia, Greece, and Egypt.

We had rehearsals at St. Paul's, and at the last rehearsal, there were camera lights.

Dr. Dawson: How were you holding up emotionally with all this stress?

Princess Diana: It was such a madcap event. I collapsed later and sobbed. Why was it a nightmare? Camilla was an undercurrent all through my engagement leading up to the wedding. You'd think Charles was marrying Camilla.

Dr. Dawson: Charles was not supportive in any way?

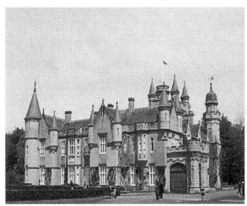 

Balmoral Castle (left). After their honeymoon cruise on Britannia, Prince Charles and Princess Diana strolled on the Balmoral Castle grounds.

Princess Diana: Almost nothing. He did send me a signet ring the night before the wedding at Clarence House. There was a note to cheer me on saying, "I'm so proud of you, and when you come up, I'll be there at the altar for you tomorrow. Just look them in the eye and knock them dead." It sounded like something you'd say to a prizefighter before the big fight.

Dr. Dawson: How were you reacting?

Princess Diana: I had a fit of bulimia the night before the wedding. My sister Jane thought it was hilarious. I was eating all I could, and I got sick, and I vomited. The next morning I was up at 5 AM. I didn't sleep that night. I felt like a guinea pig or a lamb about to be slaughtered. My freedom was over.

Dr. Dawson: How'd the wedding go for you?

Love affair and betrayal: Left: Prince Charles and his true love, Camilla, in the 1970s. Right: Camilla, Charles, Diana.

Princess Diana: The whole wedding was preposterous. My head was still at the point of being a kindergarten teacher.   But here I was getting married in this outrageous Hollywood-type production. My father went up the aisle with me. I was set to curtsey to the Queen as I'd been instructed.

Dr. Dawson: How were you feeling at the wedding?

Princess Diana: I was crazy because I was in love with Charles.   Everybody must have thought I was the luckiest girl in the world. If people only knew the truth. Charles had no intention of taking care of me.

Lady Diana and her Father Jonnie Spencer walked down the aisle at St. Paul's Cathedral, July 29th,1981.

Dr. Dawson: Where was Camilla during the wedding?

Princess Diana: I looked for her. I spotted her in her pale grey, veiled pillbox hat. On the way out of St. Paul's, I felt momentarily happy, everybody was pulling for us, cheering, and hooraying.

Everybody was happy because they assumed Charles and I were happy and in love. But I was walking into a significant role with no idea of what responsibilities were coming my way.

Princess Diana and Charles were on the Buckingham Palace balcony after their wedding.

Dr. Dawson: Where did you go from St. Paul's?

Princess Diana: Buckingham Palace. My bridesmaids and pages were holding up my long-dress train. I went to the balcony, and thousands were roaring and cheering. It was terrific. We had a wedding lunch. But Charles and I never spoke, emotionally shattered, we were exhausted.

Dr. Dawson: How'd the honeymoon come off?

Princess Diana: We went to Broadlands. Charles brought out seven novels he had not read. Laurens van der Post novels. We read them and analyzed them over lunch. We entertained top people on the *Britannia*.

Princess Diana and Charles were on the Brittania during their honeymoon.

Dr. Dawson: How did you react to all that social tension and pressure? Did your eating disorder show up?

Princess Diana: I went crazy having to socialize with all these characters. My bulimia got worse, and I ate and vomited four or five times a day on the yacht. A cycle - I ate, vomited, and got sick.

Dr. Dawson: How were your moods? Up? Down? Tranquil?

Princess Diana: I was happy one moment and crying my eyes out the next moment. My moods swung up and down. We went to Balmoral from the yacht.

Charles and Diana honeymooned at Balmoral Castle.

I was expected to adjust to being Princess of Wales instantly. But I was getting thinner and thinner. I was sicker and sicker. You mentioned Borderline Personality Disorder. What BPD symptoms are you talking about?

Dr. Dawson: Fear of abandonment is one instance. You'll improve relationships as you let go of making frantic efforts to avoid real or imagined abandonment by your husband Charles or your lovers. When you learn to stop picking the wrong man for romance, you'll defeat the problem of unstable relationships, which is another example of BPD symptoms.

You need to start seeing men realistically in the grey area and accepting some minor faults. And stop seeing men or people in the extremes – either idealizing them or demonizing them. It's called "black-and-white thinking."

To illustrate, you started marriage with Prince Charles and idealized him. Then you went to the other extreme and demonized him when he couldn't live up to your unrealistic ideals.

Men are not going to change. Don't try to change them. If you can't accept their faults at the start of a relationship, go on to the next candidate for romance.

5

Diana's marriage relationship went sideways as a function of her Borderline Personality Disorder symptoms such as extreme thinking in black and white terms – Prince Charles was an idol or idealized one moment, then demonized by Princess Diana the next moment.

Let's take a look at an example of a taped argument Diana and Charles had. Keep in mind that before this argument, thousands of conflicts between Diana and Charles were unresolved.

And buried in the subtext is the ongoing love triangle including Charles, Diana, and Camilla. Since childhood, Diana has, at times, been very stubborn, obstinate, and irrational. She was determined to force Prince Charles into a custody agreement.

Left to right: Prince Charles, Princess Diana, Charles, Camilla.

Charles: To be honest, I've never really thought about it.

Diana: Well, you wouldn't, would you?

Charles: Is there any reason why I should?

Diana: Should what?

Charles: Think about it.

Diana: Do I have to?

Charles: Is this getting us anywhere?

Diana: Not particularly, no.

Charles: Shall I just go?

Prince Charles and Princess Diana in conflict.

Diana: I don't think that would solve anything.

Charles: It may allow us to get some sleep tonight.

Diana: I couldn't sleep on this!

Charles: Quiet, you'll wake the children.

Diana: They know, anyway.

Charles: Look, three days is hardly a lifetime. Three days.

Diana: My first reaction is: what do you mean by three days?

Charles: You know full well what I mean.

Diana: Would you like to explain?

Charles: Circles, circles, round and round we go. I haven't seen anyone for days. God knows when I last picked up a newspaper or watched the TV. You make it sound as if all this is my fault. How can I explain something I don't even know?

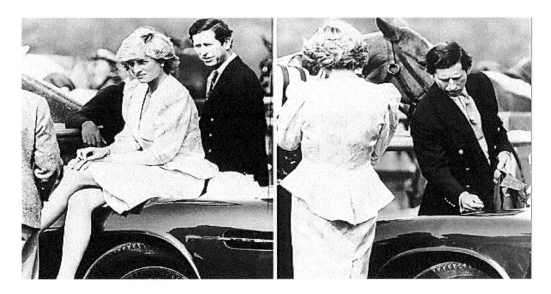

Princess Diana and Prince Charles got into a royal quarrel after Diana scratched his Aston Martin sports car.

Diana: Well, there we are. Would you like to explain further?

Charles: Not now.

Not here. Why?

Diana: I want to know. I think it needs to be resolved.

Charles: But I keep saying – why here? Are you looking for a confrontation? Honestly, I don't want or need one. I just don't want or need one.

Diana: Have you considered the implication of a custody battle?

Charles: For what?

Diana: The children.

Charles: Oh, don't be so silly. No, no, I haven't.

Diana was upset when Charles said, "Oh God, it's a boy!" when Harry was born. Charles wanted a girl.

Diana: Well, that's what would happen. The children would suffer. Do you know that?

Charles: No, no, I don't. This is so silly, talking like crazy people talking about custody. It won't come to that.

Diana: No?

Charles: No.

Diana: Well, as long as you are sure.

Charles: Please, let's not argue. Not now.

Both Prince Charles and Princess Diana were reported to be desperate to call off their wedding. But his duty to the Firm and her romantic love drove them to marry.

Diana: But that's what we are getting to because we are resolving nothing. Nothing is being decided. None of us will make a firm decision. A firm decision.

Charles: Is there one needed now? We've spent all night going over the same thing without getting anywhere, and now you're making demands for a decision? Please be sensible.

Diana: No, no, no, no, no. Let's decide it now, and then we can start afresh tomorrow morning. If nothing is decided now, we'll be in the same position tomorrow, next week, next month, as we are tonight. If there's just one godforsaken thing we can do, let's decide tonight.

Charles: I am trying to see things your way. I just can't.

Diana, Charles, and Camilla. This triangle created ongoing tension in Diana/Charles's marriage. Arguments between Diana and Charles on any topic had an underlying conflict involving the romance between Charles and Camilla.

It's too late.

Diana: Well, for once, could you put yourself out and think of me?

Charles: Don't you dare sit there and tell me to think of you. How the hell do you have the nerve to say that? I've done nothing but think of you and the children ever since this thing started.

Diana: No, no. I don't believe that at all. For once, stop being so self-centered. You still think of me as the person you married.

Charles: I stopped thinking like that years ago.

Diana spotted Camilla at her wedding. Diana was jealous and obsessed with Camilla because Charles loved Camilla, who became his second wife.

Diana: Yes, I suppose that would be a good indication of why we drifted apart, my dear.

Charles: Can I say anything, right? Tell me what it is you want me to say.

Diana: Say something I want to hear.

Charles: I'm leaving.

Diana: Oh, don't be so bloody childish.

Charles: Oh, God.

Diana: Must you always run when the pressure gets too much?

Charles: I'm not running. Unlike you, I want to deal with this like adults.

It was reported that Charles and Camilla planned to smear Diana as a mental basket case to win the public's approval.

Diana: I think I am. It's just that I want you to get it done now rather than later. I don't want it to run on like a silly soap opera.

Charles: I'm going to bed.

Diana: But why? You can sleep tomorrow. You can sleep anytime. But think of me for once, yes, think of me for once.

Charles: I'd rather think of the other parties involved. I don't know why, but right now I feel they are more important.

You'll take care of yourself; you know that.

Diana: How dare you be so presumptuous?

Charles: I'm tired.

At a party in 1989, Diana confronted Camilla saying, "I know what's going on between you and Charles and I just want you to know that.'" Camilla replied, "You've got everything you ever wanted. You've got all the men in the world fall in love with you and you've got two beautiful children, what more do you want?" The princess shot back, "I want my husband!"

Good night.

Diana: Look, you're doing it again. Come back.

For Christ's sake, come back! How can you leave it like this?

Charles: I'll speak to you tomorrow.

Diana: On no, you won't.

Charles: Good night.

Diana: Can you come in here, please?

Diana had what I'd call a BPD attitude concerning Charles – he's not trustworthy; he should cater to my desires and put me first. There is a theory of extreme BPD thinking that labels a *BPD attitude* as a **schema** – powerful beliefs that BPD people hold about themselves and the world around them.

Left: Lady Sarah Spencer, Diana's sister, Prince Charles. Right: Charles, Diana. Another romantic triangle: Sarah, Charles, and Diana.

No matter what Charles said, she'd filter it through her kind of paranoid BPD attitude. In BPD there is a **splitting** defense mechanism – people are idolized or devalued.

During her marriage to Prince Charles, Diana was distrustful. Diana listened in on phone conversations, opened Charles' mail, and hung out in hallways to overhear conversations. She overreacted because she saw people in black or white, the **splitting** defense mechanism.

Diana could not tolerate human inconsistencies and ambiguities or reconcile another's good and bad qualities into a constant, coherent understanding of that person. To Diana, Charles was all good or all evil - idolized one day, totally devalued and dismissed the next.

Diana commented on the romantic triangle involving Prince Charles, Sarah, her sister, and Diana.

Charles and Camilla - family ties

"My sister was all over him like a bad rash, and I thought, God, he must hate that. I kept out of the way. I remember being a fat, podgy, no makeup, unsmart lady, but I made a lot of noise, and he liked that, and he came up to me after dinner. We had a big dance, and he said: 'Will you show me the gallery?' and I was just about to show him the gallery and my sister Sarah comes up and tells me to push off, and I said 'At least, let me tell you where the switches are to the gallery because you won't know where they are,' and I disappeared."

"And he was charm himself and when I stood next to him the next day, a 16-year-old, for someone like that to show you any attention – I was just so sort of amazed."

Left: The Spencer family: Sarah, Charles, Diana, and Jane. Right: Sarah and Charles.

"Why would anyone like him be interested in me? That was it for about two years. Saw him off and on with Sarah and Sarah got frightfully excited about the whole thing, then she saw something different happening which I hadn't realized or twigged on to, i.e. when he had his 30th birthday dance I was asked too."

"'Why is Diana coming as well?' my sister asked. I said: 'Well, I don't know, but I'd like to come.' 'Oh, all right then,' that sort of thing. I had a lovely time at the dance – fascinating. I wasn't at all intimidated by the surroundings of Buckingham Palace. I thought, fantastic place."

"Then I was asked to stay at the de Passes in July 1980 by Philip de Pass, who is the son. 'Would you like to come and stay for a couple of nights down at Petworth because we've got the Prince of Wales staying? You're young blood; you might amuse him.' So I said, 'OK.'"

Princess Diana with her sisters, Lady Jane (left), and Lady Sarah (right).

"So I sat next to him, and Charles came in. He was all over me again, and it was bizarre. I thought, 'Well, this isn't very cool.' I thought men were supposed not to be so obvious; I thought this was very odd."

"The next minute he leaped on me practically, and I thought this was very strange, too, and I wasn't quite sure how to cope with all this. We talked about lots of things, and anyway, that was it. Frigid wasn't the word. Big F when it comes to that. He said: 'You must come to London with me tomorrow. I've got to work at Buckingham Palace; you must come to work with me.' I thought this was too much."

"I said: 'No, I can't.' I thought, 'How will I explain my presence at Buckingham Palace when I'm supposed to be staying with Philip?' Then he asked me to Cowes on *Britannia,* and he had lots of older friends there, and I was somewhat intimidated, but they were all over me like a bad rash. I felt very strange about the whole thing - somebody was talking."

Prince Harry and Meghan were tempted by a $7 million Malibu mansion.

"I came in and out, in and out, then I went to stay with my sister Jane at Balmoral, where Robert Fellowes, Jane's husband, was assistant private secretary to the Queen. I was terrified – shitting bricks. I was frightened because I had never stayed at Balmoral, and I wanted to get it right. The anticipation was worse than actually being there."

"I was all right once I got in through the front door. I had a normal single bed! I have always done my packing and unpacking – I was always appalled that Prince Charles takes 22 pieces of hand luggage with him. That's before the other stuff. I have four or five. I felt rather embarrassed."

"I stayed back at the castle because of the press interest. It was considered a good idea. Mr. and Mrs. Parker-Bowles were there at all my visits. I was the youngest there by a long way. Charles used to ring me up and say: 'Would you like to come for a walk, come for a barbeque?' So I said: 'Yes, please.' I thought this was all wonderful."

Meghan Markle, with Prince Harry, wants to be the unofficial king and queen of the USA.

Courtship: "Then it sort of built up from there, then the press seized upon it. Later that became simply unbearable in our flat, but my three girls were wonderful, star performers, loyalty beyond belief. The feeling was I wish Prince Charles would hurry up and get on with it. The Queen was fed up. Then Charles rang me up from Klosters and said, 'I've got something to ask you.' Instinct in a female, you know what's coming. Anyway, I sat up all night with my girls, saying, 'What do I say, what do I do?' bearing in mind that there's somebody else around."

Proposal: Diana then got together with Charles, and she detailed it: "'Will you marry me?' I laughed. I remember thinking, 'This is a joke,' and I said, 'Yeah, OK,' and laughed. He was deadly serious. He said: 'You do realize that one day you will be Queen.' And a voice said to me inside: 'You won't be Queen, but you'll have a tough role.'"

After Meghan Markle's "two-year itch," Prince Harry and Meghan are blowing off royal duties, maybe buying a mansion in Malibu, California, and claiming to jet between Canada and the UK. They expect to make millions selling the royal brand in Hollywood and elsewhere.

"So I thought 'OK,' so I said: 'Yes.' I said: 'I love you so much, I love you so much.' He said: 'Whatever love means.' He said it then. So I thought that was great. I thought he meant that! And so he ran upstairs and rang his mother."

Press harassment: "Then it all started to build up, sort of like the press were unbearable following my every move," Diana complained. "I understood they had a job, but people did not realize they had binoculars on me the whole time. They hired the opposite flat in Old Brompton Road, which was a library which looked into my bedroom, and it wasn't fair on the girls. I couldn't put the telephone off the hook in case any of their family were ill in the night. The papers used to ring me up at 2 AM – they were just putting out another story – 'Could I confirm or deny it?'"

Meghan Markle, Hollywood TV actress.

Princess Diana was discussing her interest in Prince Charles from the age of 16. She covered the courtship, proposal, and press harassment. Diana was somewhat naïve about the consequences of marrying Prince Charles. Prince Charles was pressured by The Firm, the senior royals, to hurry and get married to an appropriate young virgin from aristocratic circles.

However, Charles was in love with Camilla. Charles pretended to be in love with Diana. To make it work, both Diana and Charles needed shallow expectations going into their marriage.

Besides Diana and Charles crossing the lines of the expected royal roles, today, Meghan Markle, Prince Harry, and Prince Andrew have upset royal traditions.

Meghan Markle and Kate Middleton, two very different women.

Markle, the Duchess of Sussex, left the UK for Canada after Prince Harry and Meghan announced they would step back from their roles as senior members of the royal family. Markle seems to make significant changes every two years. Her first marriage ended after two years. Markle married actor and producer Trevor Engelson in 2011. They divorced in 2013.

Meghan married Prince Harry in 2018 – in 2020, two years later, they rejected the usual royal role, claimed they'd live in Canada and the UK. However, Meghan and Harry are looking to buy a mansion in Malibu, California. They can then exploit their royal brand for money in Hollywood and worldwide in commercial markets.

Left: Prince Andrew was struggling, in a media interview, to explain this photo with a girl, 17, who claimed Jeffrey Epstein and Ghislaine Maxwell trafficked her to Prince Andrew for three sexual encounters. Right: In 2010, Prince Andrew strolled through New York's Central Park with Epstein after he'd done jail time for sex offenses.

In two years, by 2022, I'd expect Meghan and Prince Harry to start another chapter after Markle gets her "two-year itch," such as have a three-picture deal with a major studio. Plus, endorsement deals worth many millions. Of course, they'll promote charities and climate change while jet-setting around the world on exotic vacations and enjoying a luxury lifestyle.

Before marrying Prince Harry, Markle played the race card to explain her lack of success as an actress. She said, "Being ethnically ambiguous, as I was pegged in the industry, meant I could audition for virtually any role. Sadly, it didn't matter. I wasn't black enough for the black roles, and I wasn't white enough for the white ones, leaving me somewhere in the middle as the ethnic chameleon who couldn't book a job."

Since success in Hollywood is a crapshoot, she can't be blamed for not being an A-list actress. But with her royal marriage to Prince Harry, Markle can now get A-list treatment.

Prince Andrew caught up in the Epstein criminal case, has made a mistake in talking to the press. Prince Andrew, following a disastrous television interview with the British Broadcasting Corporation over his ties to Mr. Epstein, said late last year he would cooperate with law enforcement agencies in their investigations into the disgraced financier and his associates.

Prince Andrew should get a criminal lawyer and not comment on the Epstein case. He's presumed innocent unless convicted of a crime. Prince Andrew, the Duke of York, will step away from his public duties as a royal following the fallout from his past friendship with the late sex offender Jeffrey Epstein. Prince Andrew said his association with Epstein had disrupted his royal duties. He said, "Therefore, I have asked Her Majesty if I may step back from public duties for the foreseeable future, and she has given her permission."

6

Princess Diana discussed her honeymoon, pregnancy, and the birth of William in this chapter. She was experiencing BPD symptoms such as bulimia, mood swings, depression, and a suicidal attempt or gesture.

Her struggles included coping with the demands of being Princess of Wales, attending public functions, private social gatherings, and yet being sick much of the time. Prince Charles was not supportive of her viewpoint.

He felt inadequate to deal with her bulimia and volatile emotions. His response was to show her coldness, become frustrated, and escape by riding his polo pony.

Diana, 20, waited for the half a shandy she ordered on board the Britannia when she visited the officers' mess. A shandy is a beer mixed with a sweet-soft drink.

Dr. Dawson: Tell me more about the honeymoon.

Princess Diana: One change was that people coming to Balmoral called me "Your Royal Highness," or "Ma'am" and they curtseyed. I treated everybody the same and avoided getting uppity, pretentious, or snobbish.

My romantic illusions shattered into the reality that marriage to Charles was boring. We were cruising the Mediterranean on the *Britannia*. Charles would rather read a novel than have sex with me. I was feeling sexually inadequate on our honeymoon.

Of course, Charles was trotting around in the rear, constantly calling Camilla to get coaching on how to handle his new marriage. Right away, I could see Charles was not trustworthy.

A kilted Prince Charles gazed at his kingdom at Balmoral Castle in 1978 (left). Charles and Diana on their honeymoon at Balmoral.

Dr. Dawson: What did Charles do at Balmoral on your honeymoon?

Princess Diana: He went for long walks, sat on top of the highest hill at Balmoral, and ogled, rubbernecked, and gazed at his kingdom. Sometimes he'd read to me.

He read those Laurens van der Post novels or Jung. I did tapestry. Anything to keep Charles busy, so he wasn't chasing his mistress.

Dr. Dawson: How did interactions go with the royal family?

Britain's Queen Elizabeth II, Prince Philip sit at Balmoral with their children Princess Anne (L), Prince Charles (R), and the new-born Prince Andrew (C) playing with a corgi on September 8th, 1960 (left). The Royal Family at Balmoral, including Princess Diana (right).

Princess Diana: I stupidly thought that a man's wife came first. But when the Queen, the Queen Mother, Prince Philip, Prince Andrew, Princess Anne, and Princess Margaret – Margo visited Balmoral, Charles rushed around to cater to them first. They all came ahead of me, his wife!

Dr. Dawson: Sounds like you were developing a sense of entitlement. What did Charles do?

Prince Charles is playing polo and fishing in Scotland.

Princess Diana: It was, "Daddy, care for a biscuit and tea?" Or "Mummy, can I fix you a little drink?" Then it's "Granny, can I get you a beverage?" "Margo, a gin and tonic?" "Anne, can I get you a veggie juice?" "Andrew, a martini?"

Then after every guest, including the butler, has been served, once in a while, he'll ask, "Duch, can I get you aspirin for your headache?" Charles had a knack for passive-aggressive zingers, digs, and insults. "Duch" is my nickname.

Breaches of the no-touching rule occur all the time with the royals (left). Prince Charles and Princess Diana appeared sad and stressed-out (right).

Dr. Dawson: What is the underlying conflict about from your perspective?

Princess Diana: The main problem with the marriage to Charles was that it was a deception. I was deceived, misled, and betrayed.

I didn't realize that Charles was setting up an arranged marriage of convenience to move the monarchy or the Firm forward at my expense. It was a covertly arranged marriage. I was expecting a loving companion and babies like a healthy marriage.

Pictured are Princess Diana with secret lover James Hewitt (left). She presented him with a polo award. Camilla and Prince Charles.

Dr. Dawson: What was his motivation?

Princess Diana: His aim was just a loveless marriage of convenience to produce an heir – William - and a spare – Harry. He intended to be King. I wanted a husband who loved me. He'd open his diary, and photos of Camilla would tumble out.

I did the best I could and put up a socially acceptable front by telling the press, "Married life is wonderful." What was the purpose of the honeymoon? My husband's focus: A) his books; B) his fishing pole; C) his friends in his club.

Prince Charles, Princess Diana, Nancy Reagan, and President Reagan.

Dr. Dawson: What about your friends? Your books? Your hobbies?

Princess Diana: The Prince of Wales thought he was above my interests and my friends. To Charles, my friends and interests were nutty, loopy, daft, and silly.

Dr. Dawson: You were showing symptoms of bulimia, depression, somewhat suicidal, and ready to cut your wrists in that August to October window. What treatment did you get?

Princess Diana, Princess-of-Wales, pregnant and on a tour in April 1982 (left). Kate Middleton and Princess Diana in maternity fashion.

Princess Diana: I went down to London, and a series of doctors, psychiatrists, and analysts examined, scrutinized, and inspected me and judged that I'd lost my mind. They got me loaded on psychiatric meds like Valium and various pills. Case closed.

The royals assumed that Diana had been handled, treated, and cured. Now Diana wouldn't come screeching out of the darkness waving a butcher knife and slashing Camilla and Charles as they cuddle in bed – like a scene from an American-horror movie.

Dr. Dawson: What happened in October?

Prince Charles and Princess Diana at a ball on October 30th, 1985 (left). Princess Diana in 1981 at a formal social event.

Princess Diana: I was pregnant with William. And then I had to do a tour of Wales for several days putting on the Princess and Prince of Wales show to entertain everybody.

I gave a speech in Welsh. It was scary because I was frightened of the crowds, and yet Charles was pushing me to get out of the car and meet the public.

Dr. Dawson: How was the bulimia and morning sickness?

A pregnant Princess Diana chatted with Prince Charles during a polo event at Windsor (left). Princess Diana pregnant with William (right) at another polo event.

Princess Diana: I was sicker than a dog with bulimia and morning sickness. All I felt like doing was vomiting. Do you know how I looked? I was grey, drab, melancholy, gaunt, emaciated, and thin. How was my energy level? I was exhausted, couldn't sleep, couldn't eat, and had no energy. Yet I had to do my royal duty.

Dr. Dawson: Must have been tough to have to carry on with your Princess of Wales' duties while you were sick.

Both Princess Diana and Kate Middleton appeared too thin.   Princess Diana and Prince Charles - Charles is holding William.

Princess Diana: This whole period was hell. I'd have on this evening gown at some formal social event at Balmoral, Sandringham, or Windsor, and I was continually dashing out to faint or was sick and vomiting. Then I'd prance back into the polo ball or charity extravaganza to be the graceful, delightful Princess of Wales in the spotlight.

Dr. Dawson: The meds didn't help you?

Shown are Princess Diana with the Queen and the royal family at the formal christening of William.

Princess Diana: All the time, I was pressured to pop more pills, and I just refused at some point. I'd rather be sick. Everybody gave their sympathy to Charles. Oh my god! The poor Prince of Wales has to put up with this ridiculous creature Diana with all her problems!

Dr. Dawson: How did you handle your duties while you were sick?

Pictured are Princess Diana, John Travolta (left). Diana, age 19, wore a black Emanuel evening gown in 1981 (right).

Princess Diana: I'd dash out during some ultra-formal, black-tie, and black-dress party celebrating God knows what and puke. I'd go back and stand around, meeting people out of duty. Then some royals would grumble that if I was sick, I should just go to bed. I couldn't win.

Dr. Dawson: Then you made a suicidal gesture or attempt at Sandringham?

Princess Diana threw herself down a staircase in a suicide gesture or cry for help. While Diana was pregnant, she was often sick with morning sickness, depression, and anxiety.

Princess Diana: I'd gotten into a horrible row – a verbal fight with Charles. He was complaining about my sickness. His attitude was that I was just faking it and crying wolf. He announced, "I'm not going to listen. You're always bothering me with this nonsense. I'm going riding!" And off he went riding.

Dr. Dawson: What did you do then?

Princess Diana complained that Prince Charles (left) abandoned her when she was sick to play polo. Prince William (right) and Prince Harry followed in the family tradition and played polo.

Princess Diana: I threw myself down the stairs. The Queen came rushing out, shaking, and frightened. She was afraid I was going to lose the baby because I was quite bruised around the stomach. When Charles came back from riding, he just removed himself from the situation.

Dr. Dawson: Did a doctor examine you after you threw yourself down the stairs?

Princess Diana gave birth to William.

Princess Diana: I was checked up by a doctor and had only minor scrapes and bruises. Doctors were called to give me sedatives and more pills. The royals wanted to keep my body in shape for reproduction.

I was using food and bulimia to comfort myself in the face of my husband's coldness. I was just dismissed as some result of raging hormones, crazy and rampant bulimia, and suicidal sulking.

Dr. Dawson: Maybe you were channeling or directing your anger and frustration into your eating disorder. Compulsive eating and vomiting. How do you see it?

After Diana had her children, her marriage fell apart more rapidly. Charles chased after Camilla.

Princess Diana: After all the shrinks and doctors and analysts, I guess what I've understood is that I was taking an emotional detour around my problems.

But I had morning sickness, which led to a lot of talk about me because I was looking emaciated, gaunt, skinny, and wasted. I didn't feel like eating. And when I did eat, I vomited it up.

Dr. Dawson: How did William's birth go?

Princess Diana felt excluded at Prince William's christening. She was sick in bed.

Princess Diana: They wanted a Caesarean, but I wasn't told. I went through a terrible labor period. The press was hounding me about when I was going to have the baby. William was induced.

I finally gave birth to a boy. Then I had postnatal depression. I went through hell because Charles was always undependable. He was off on his polo pony when I needed him.

Dr. Dawson: How did the christening work?

Princess Diana: In August 1982, William's christening went off. They were taking photos of William with the Queen, Queen Mother, and Charles. I was in bed, sobbing, crying, and whimpering. I was going from panic to depression to self-pity and back.

7

Diana was stressed-out by an ongoing romantic triangle between herself, Prince Charles, and Camilla. She was also upset because her affair with James Hewitt was ending. On the positive side, Princess Diana got support from her mother, Frances.

She attended a party for Camilla Parker Bowles' sister, Annabel Elliot. Prince Charles was against her attendance because Camilla would be there. But Diana insisted on attending. During the party, Diana noticed Charles and Camilla had vanished. So she wandered around the party and located Charles and Camilla, who were off having a private conversation.

Diana then confronted them – told them she knew what was going on between them. Charles, Camilla, and Diana then circulated the party as if nothing happened. Of course, on the ride home, Charles and Diana were hostile to each other.

Photos of Princess Diana and James Hewitt.

The combination of the Charles/Camilla issue and Diana's love affair ups and downs, such as breaking up with James Hewitt, resulted in Diana experiencing some Borderline Personality Disorder symptoms. Her BPD indicators included roller-coaster emotions, wide mood swings, explosive bouts of anger, rage, and worries about abandonment.

A theoretical variable in the possible cause of BPD is early separation or loss and ineffective parenting. I think Diana's parents did the best they could. But it was reported that, while Diana and her mother were close, by the end of her life, Diana was giving her mother the silent treatment. Princess Diana commonly cut off or ghosted most people sooner or later. Ghosting is having someone that you believe cares about you, whether it be a friend or someone you are dating, disappear from contact without any explanation at all. No phone call or email, not even a text.

Left: Senior royal women – Princess Margaret, the Queen Mother, and Queen Elizabeth. Right: Princess Diana sharing her marriage troubles in public on TV.

The senior royals were against Diana's public discussions of her marriage problems. Princess Margaret destroyed letters Diana had sent to the Queen Mother. I think the senior royals, The Firm, has a good point. But I realize Diana's popularity is partly connected to her open attitude about sharing her issues.

Diana was a beautiful, warm-hearted lady who did a lot of charity work. She helped the less fortunate, including homeless alcoholics and drug addicts, and those with various medical problems. She said she overcame her eating disorders later in life. However, Diana continued to struggle with love relationships.

Because Prince Charles loved Camilla and continued his affair with her, it is no surprise that Diana had revenge romances. She had romantic adventures with Barry Mannakee 1987, James Hewitt 1991, Oliver Hoare 1992, James Gilbey 1994, Will Carling 1994, Hasnat Khan 1995, and Dodi Fayed, who died with Diana in 1997.

Left: Diana, Dodi Fayed. Right: Prince Charles joked with James Hewitt and Diana. Charles knew Diana was having a sex affair with Hewitt – Prince Charles did not care.

Diana was sensitive and compassionate, probably reacted severely to her parents' divorce, and she expected too much from Prince Charles. The Firm pressured Prince Charles to hurry up and find an aristocratic virgin bride. Camilla didn't fit the requirements. So what could Charles do? And Diana was a naïve young woman who expected a marriage based on true romance and love.

Diana's marriage to Charles, however, suffered due to their incompatibility and extramarital affairs. The couple separated in 1992, soon after the breakdown of their relationship became public knowledge. The details of their marital difficulties became increasingly publicized, and the marriage ended in divorce in 1996.

Diana got romantically attached to her married bodyguard, Barry Mannakee, in 1987. Mannakee, 14 years older than Diana, was a father figure for her. Barry later died in a car crash – Diana said the security service set up the crash to cover up what Mannakee knew about Diana and Prince Charles which sounds paranoid.

Left: Princess Diana and her lover, Oliver Hoare. Right: Diana, Prince Charles, and Hoare. Diana made malicious phone calls to dashing art dealer Hoare, who was married.

James Hewitt, one of Princess Diana's lovers, said Diana was a suspicious and demanding woman. She sent him many love letters and called him ten times a day; he monetized his relationship with Diana - he wrote a tell-all book about their sex affair called *Love and War*.

James Gilbey, another one of Diana's lovers, was caught on tape telling Diana he loved her in a pre-1990 phone call and called her two affectionate nicknames: Squidgy and Squidge. The incident was called Squidgygate or Dianagate by the media; their romance reached its peak in 1989. Gilbey was a former actor and car salesman.

The Gilbey-Diana tape revealed him saying, "And so, darling, what other lows today?" To which Princess Diana replied, "I was terrible at lunch, and I nearly started blubbing..."

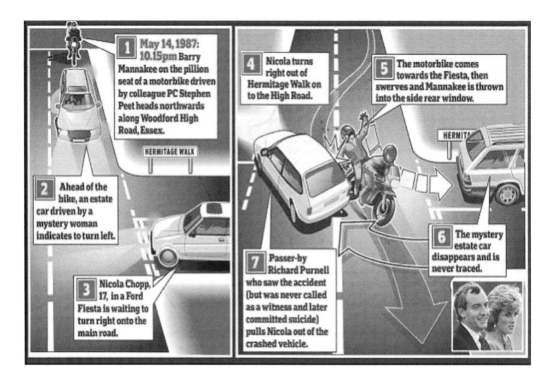

Diagram of the crash that killed Barry Mannakee, the married bodyguard who Diana fell in love with – she suspected he was murdered.

"I just felt so sad and empty and thought bloody hell; after all, I've done for this fucking family. It's just so desperate. Always being innuendo, the fact that I'm going to do something dramatic because I wouldn't say I like the confines of this marriage. Charles makes my real-life torture!"

Prince Charles and Camilla Parker Bowles initially met and began their romantic relationship in the 1970s. They then carried on an affair into the 1980s and 1990s while they were each married to other people. Tapes surfaced of an infamous Charles/Camilla conversation at bedtime – called Camillagate.

Diana's lovers who helped her cope with Prince Charles/Camilla's affair. Top row: James Hewitt, James Gilbey, Dodi Fayed. Bottom row: Barry Mannakee, Will Carling, and Hasnat Khan.

In the tapes, the prince said to Camilla, "Oh God. I'll live inside your trousers or something. It would be much easier!"

To which she responds, "What are you going to turn into, a pair of knickers? Oh, you're going to come back as a pair of knickers. He then tells her, "Or, God forbid, a Tampax. Just my luck!"

The two then joked about him being a whole box of tampons for her. When the recordings were leaked to the press, the future monarch's entire family was distraught and disgusted by the entire thing.

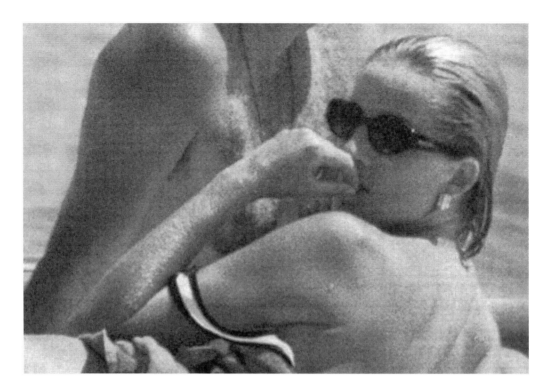

Princess Diana pictured with Dodi Al-Fayed. At the time, she was heartbroken by her break-up with Hasnat Khan.

What is the significance of Dr. Hasnat Khan and Dodi Fayed, who had love affairs with Princess Diana? They both came from radically different Islamic cultures and religions compared to Diana's background. Khan's parents rejected Diana because they wanted their son to marry a nice Pakistani woman.

Diana met Hasnat Khan in a hospital; she smuggled him into the palace in the trunk of a car. She went to his apartment, ironed his shirts, and cooked him dinner. Khan said when he was out at a pub with Diana, the Princess wanted to order drinks – because she'd never done that before.

Left: Princess Diana, Hasnat Khan. Right: Khan's new love.

She claimed she was ready to run away with Hasnat and live with him in Pakistan. Diana got carried away in her romances. Diana demanded that Hasnat Khan must go public with his love and affair with her. She was suffocating him with her attention and ultimatums. Dodi Fayed was another Arab or Middle Eastern guy Diana had a fling with before her death. After her divorce from Charles and her split with Hasnat Khan, she connected with Fayed. Dodi was the son of a wealthy Egyptian. Fayed had a reputation as a playboy who was a Hollywood movie producer.

There were rumors that Diana was aiming to make Hasnat Khan jealous by dating Dodi. Dodi's father asserted the car crash, that killed his son and Diana, was a conspiracy by British spies from MI-6 because she was about to marry Dodi, a Muslim. Mohamed Al-Fayed has attempted to preserve an idealistic, lasting impression of his version of the relationship between Diana and his late son.

Left: A scene from a movie based on Diana's affair with Hasnat Khan. Right: Khan, Diana's former lover – he said the film *Diana* was a betrayal of their love.

How did Princess Diana get involved with Hasnat Khan? Two years earlier, her life had changed when she had gone to see her friend and nurse turned acupuncturist, Oonagh Toffalo's husband Joseph, who was in a hospital. He was recovering from heart surgery at the Brompton Road Hospital.

One day while she was visiting Joseph, in walked a doctor who, according to reports, begun intently talking to the patient about his prognosis, totally ignoring the blonde woman sitting next to the bed. When he left the room, Diana reportedly turned to her friend and exclaimed, "Oonagh, isn't he drop-dead gorgeous?"

He was Dr. Hasnat Khan, a Pakistani heart surgeon from a very traditional family from Lahore. The duo could not have been more dissimilar.

Left to right: James Gilbey, Oliver Hoare, James Hewitt, Will Carling, and Barry Mannakee. These men were Diana's lovers.

He worked non-stop and was committed to his career. His long hours meant his one-bedroom apartment was, according to reports, a mess. Out of shape, he loved greasy takeout chicken. She was the most famous woman in the world who could have dated or been romanced by pretty much any man. But the man she wanted was a somewhat geeky, fat doctor who smoked.

The odd duo's first date could not have been further from Diana's glamorous life: it was a trip to visit his aunt and uncle to pick up some books. When Khan was interviewed by British police years later before the official inquest into her death, he said of that outing: "I did not think for one minute that she would say yes, but I asked her if she would like to come with me. I was shocked when she said she would."

Diana's lovers were labeled with nicknames: Babby Mannakee, the father figure; James Hewitt, the cad; Will Carling, the rugby captain; James Gilbey, the old friend.

For the next two years, the couple had a clandestine, on-off relationship, managing to keep their romance out of the press. According to reports, theirs was a very ordinary existence, something that Diana had craved for years.

They went to the pub and had drinks, they spent time at a jazz club, he would come around to her Kensington Palace apartment, and they would have take-away. To make Khan feel comfortable in her home, she converted a spare room in her apartment into a den for him where he could watch soccer and kickback.

After the film *Diana* was released, Khan said it was a betrayal of his love for Princess Diana. "I can see a lot of humor in a lot of bad things, but in this one, I can't," Khan remarked. "I haven't seen the film, and I haven't met anyone who has seen it, but I can tell you for sure that it's based on a superficial idea. I have kept things very discreet, but now this film is trying to open things up again."

Left to right: Diana, Dodi Fayed, Hasnat Khan, Diana. Dodi was an Egyptian Muslim; Khan was a Pakistani Muslim. Princess Diana was a lip service Anglican, baptized into the Church of England - she was not compatible with these men or any of her lovers.

Princess Diana's oppositional romantic behavior broke boundaries and was a disaster for her. First, she got involved with Prince Charles, who did not love her and who was in love with Camilla. Next, she got involved with a series of inappropriate men, who were sometimes married, from different social classes, and some were from different religious and cultural backgrounds.

Diana had an affair with James Hewitt from 1986 to 1991. The first boundary she broke was that she was married to Prince Charles, the heir apparent to the throne of the United Kingdom. Hewitt was from a middle-class background – Diana was from an aristocratic, upper-class. James was assigned to be Diana's riding instructor. James, an army officer, betrayed Diana by trying to sell 64 love letters she sent him and writing a tell-all book.

Left: Prince Harry. Center: James Hewitt. Right: Diana. Although Harry looks like Hewitt, Hewitt said he is not the father.

Barry Mannakee, Diana's bodyguard, a police officer from the Royal Protection Squad, had a sex affair with Princess Diana while he was married with two children. They were involved from 1984 to 1986. He was transferred to the Diplomatic Protection Squad after his supervisors determined his relationship with Diana was inappropriate.

In 1987 he died in a crash involving a car and the motorcycle he was riding. Diana said he was bumped off – murdered, which sounds overly suspicious. She said it was the most significant blow to her life and that she was only happy when he was around.

Oliver Hoare had an affair with Diana in 1992. He was an art dealer who was married to a woman from a wealthy French oil family and had three kids.

Princess Diana was said to be one of the more than 1,500 beauties with Spain's scandal-scarred former King Juan Carlos enjoyed sex romps, and the randy royal has become tangled in a new kickback and money-laundering probe!

James Gilbey went from acting to work behind the camera. Gilbey was a Lotus car salesman who was heir to a gin fortune. He became famous concerning Diana when sensational tapes surfaced – known as Squidgygate – which revealed risque chat with Princess Diana and Gilbey. Their sex affair was reportedly in 1994 – although they'd known each other for over a decade.

Gilbey stood Diana up for a date once. In retaliation, Diana got revenge by mixing a flour-and-egg paste and pouring it on his Alpha Romeo sports car – which ruined the paint job. Diana was not the angel she is often portrayed as in the media.

Diana's lovers helped her cope with her break-up with Prince Charles. Left to right: James Gilbey, Oliver Hoare, James Hewitt, Will Carling, Barry Manakee, Princess Diana.

Will Carling, a former rugby player, married, was linked to Princess Diana as a lover in 1994.

Hasnat Khan was in a romance with Princess Diana from 1995 to 1997. Khan is a heart surgeon. Diana claimed he was the love of her life and called him Mr. Wonderful. However, he was from a very different Pakistani culture/religion, and his parents rejected Diana as a potential wife.

Khan did not want the media attention Diana brought to their relationship. Later, Khan married an Afgan woman who he divorced a couple of years later.

Dodi Fayed, a film producer and the son of billionaire Mohamed Al-Fayed, was involved with Diana in July of 1997 and died in a car crash with Diana on August 31st, 1997. Fayed, like Diana, was an unstable character and a cocaine addict.

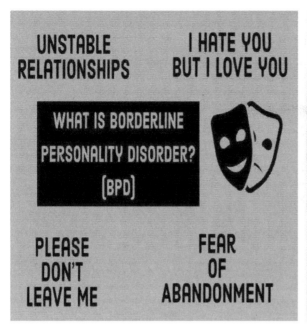 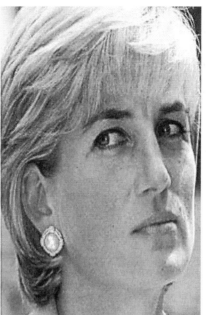

Some BPD characteristics Diana experienced are shown.

In 1986, Fayed married model Suzanne Gregard, but the couple divorced after only eight months of marriage. In July 1997, Fayed became romantically involved with Diana, Princess of Wales. Earlier that summer, Fayed had become engaged to an American model, Kelly Fisher, and had bought a house in Malibu, California, for himself and Fisher with money from his father.

Fisher subsequently claimed Fayed had jilted her for Diana and filed a breach of contract suit against him, claiming that he had "led her emotionally up to the altar and abandoned her when they were almost there. He threw her love away in a cruel way, with no regard for her whatsoever." She dropped the lawsuit shortly after Fayed's death. Fayed's father claimed British spies murdered his son and Diana because Dodi was a Muslim.

Princess Diana seemed happy one moment, then depressed, or angry, or paranoid the next moment. BPD seemed to stimulate her volatile emotions and madcap love life.

In conclusion, Princess Diana had a series of lovers demonstrating her Borderline Personality Disorder (BPD) symptoms and her inability to find a man for a significant, lasting romance leading to marriage.

Why did Diana's BPD interfere with her aim to find her true love? BPD was initially developed as a mental disorder category because it seemed to be on the borderline with bipolar disorder, schizophrenia, and various anxiety disorders. Diana had an unstable self-image and crazy mood swings. You can think of BPD as a kind of immature teenage stage involving crazy feelings, lovesick fantasies, and panic if one is rejected or abandoned in a romantic relationship.

She panicked when rejected or if Diana perceived abandonment. So, she could not sustain romantic relationships. Diana had ongoing feelings of loneliness, boredom, emptiness, and a spiritual hole inside her. Symptoms included impulsive behavior, binge-eating, and self-mutilation.

8

Princess Diana went through a painful process of adjustment in completing her royal duties as Princess of Wales. In this chapter, she revealed her husband was jealous of the astonishing popularity that Princess Diana experienced. On royal duties and in foreign travel, crowds and thousands of press people wanted to see her and not Charles.

She continued to have bulimic, self-destructive (cutting), and suicidal problems. Her mental disorder symptoms point to ongoing Borderline Personality Disorder (BPD). BPD symptoms include:

- **Behavioral:** antisocial behavior, compulsive behavior, hostility, impulsivity, irritability, risk-taking actions, self-destructive behavior, self-harm, social isolation, or lack of restraint
- **Mood:** anger, anxiety, general discontent, guilt, loneliness, mood swings, or sadness
- **Psychological:** depression, distorted self-image, grandiosity, or narcissism
- **Also frequently:** thoughts of suicide

Princess Diana had a love affair with James Hewitt (left). Prince Charles eventually went public and admitted his relationship with Camilla. Charles, Prince of Wales and Camilla, Duchess of Cornwall (right).

Both Charles and Diana went public with their love affairs: Charles and Camilla; Diana admitted a romance with James Hewitt. She revealed that behind the glamorous façade, her life was in ruins, and she had no sex life.

Dr. Dawson: How was married life as the Princess of Wales?

Princess Diana: It took me six or seven years to relax into the role of Princess Diana. I was very timid, shy, and fearful of carrying out the duties of being the Princess of Wales. I helped write thank-you letters for all the wedding presents.

Diana in a Catherine Walker design (left). Princess Diana in a Bruce Oldfield designer dress (right).

Charles's private secretary recruited some ladies-in-waiting to help out. I was too panicked to develop a sense of adventure, and so I clung to Charles as far as engagements and royal-social functions.

Dr. Dawson: What else did you deal with as Princess of Wales?

Princess Diana: Contrary to what people assumed, I had no wardrobe when I married Charles. I was not a fashion freak and did not collect designer items.

Princess Diana wore Versace in Sydney in 1996 (left). In 1982, Diana made the tailored suit with padded shoulders a hit.

I only had one formal dress, one acceptable skirt, and one stylish pair of shoes. Mummy and I had to rush around, buying 17 versions of every clothing item.

Dr. Dawson: What was the big problem with clothes?

Princess Diana: Because I needed to change clothing five or more times a day, I was required to show the spot-on taste in clothing outfits to fit various seasons, months, holidays, types of social engagements, charity balls, and parties.

Diana, Charles, and William received tumultuous welcomes on royal tours. But Prince Charles got jealous because the crowds wanted to see Princess Diana and not him. At right, Princess Diana greeted crowds of fans in 1982.

Luckily my sisters had worked at *Vogue*, and I was able to come up with a contact there who helped me select various items I needed.

Dr. Dawson: You finally got the proper clothing, so then you felt adequate?

Princess Diana: Finally. Later I got some contacts in the fashion industry I could call for advice. I had to find designers with clothing that would be practical and yet stylish.

Princess Diana and Prince Charles on a Royal Tour in Australia and New Zealand in 1983.

It was essential to have useful items in demure colors and modest necklines. I started out wearing froufrou princess clothes I felt The Firm would approve of or that Charles would find sexy.

Dr. Dawson: But as your self-identity, your sense of self improved, you had less need to people-please, and lost your high need for approval. I take it your clothing styles reflected your inner psychological and self-concept growth?

Princess Diana greeted enthusiastic crowds during a 1983 Royal Tour of New Zealand and Australia. Because she had become a media star, Prince Charles grew tense and angry when she was the focus of attention.

Princess Diana: As I got more confident, I got more into trendy designer styles a society girl might wear. The more famous I got and the more frantic media attention I got, the more Charles ignored me.

Dr. Dawson: Why was a wardrobe such a challenge?

Princess Diana: It was one surprise after another. Some tricks were to have weights in hems so that my skirts would not blow up in the wind. Suddenly I had to look stylish, discreet, and royal.

I was under the press, public, and monarchy scrutiny to look royal, classy, and not appear dated or looking like a hooker. Royal engagements and tours were a nightmare.

Dr. Dawson: How so?

Princess Diana: I was constantly blowing it. I was changing shape because I was pregnant with William. I'd put on clothes that suddenly did not fit.

Then I'd have to rush off to give a speech someplace while I was scared to death and my dress was tearing at the seams. Domestic engagements were the worst.

Princess Diana created an explosive reaction on Royal Tours. She delighted crowds of fans.

Dr. Dawson: Any other amusing conflicts?

Princess Diana: Many. At a play, I was wearing a fake fur coat, and the anti-fur activists were screaming at me. I never wore it again. Bombers were tossing bombs at me. I had to take a unique driving course and be accompanied by a police officer. So I had to make further adjustments to take care of the policeman.

Dr. Dawson: How about foreign tours?

Princess Diana had a charismatic touch, which was revealed on Royal Tours such as this 1983 Australia and New Zealand trip. Tension mounted between Diana and Charles as the crowds called out to Diana and were less into him.

Princess Diana: We took this six-week tour of Australia and New Zealand – Charles, baby William, and me. The problem was that there was this explosion with incredible crowds of people and thousands of press. The tension between Charles and me intensified to insane levels because he was jealous of the attention paid to me.

Dr. Dawson: Why was he so jealous?

Princess Diana charmed the people of New Zealand and Australia on a Royal Tour.

Princess Diana: Everybody kept asking to see me and not him. They wanted to check out my clothing and see how I handled myself. Charles was fighting with me because he was jealous that I was this sudden-media star.

I argued with him that it was not my fault and I hadn't asked for this. Any woman he'd marry would get the same treatment. He wanted to be the star of the show and threw fits about it.

Princess Diana greeted well-wishers during her trip to a park in Burnaby, Canada, May 6th, 1986.

Dr. Dawson: Any other foreign trips?

Princess Diana: We flew around Europe – Hungary, Italy, Portugal, and Spain. I met with the Pope – Pope John Paul II. Our communication broke down. I asked him how his wounds were since he had recently been shot.

He interpreted wrong and assumed I was pregnant and talking about my womb. Wounds misinterpreted as the womb. The King and Queen of Spain focused on Charles. I was running to the toilet and vomiting because my bulimia was impossible.

Princess Diana and Prince Charles are pictured on a Royal Tour of Canada in 1983 (left). Princess Diana is shown during the Royal visit to Australia for the Bicentenary celebrations on January 29th, 1988 (right).

Dr. Dawson: Then Harry came along, and how did that come off?

Princess Diana: Somehow, I got pregnant with Harry. I guess Charles took a break from scrunching Camilla. When Harry was born, Charles was disappointed because he wanted a girl.

Dr. Dawson: How was your bulimic problem? Better, I hope?

Princess Diana: I had bouts with bulimia. The Queen told me that my bulimia was appalling to Charles, and that caused our marriage problems.

Princess Diana led Prince William on a pony at Highgrove.

My bulimia was a symptom caused by Charles, who was a block of ice. He didn't love me, he cheated on me with Camilla, and was an all-around bastard.

Dr. Dawson: How did Charles cope with your bulimia and other psychological symptoms? Did he continue to be cold?

Princess Diana: At times, I would try to shock Charles to get some concern or a reaction from him. Once I grabbed a penknife and scratched and cut myself on my chest and thighs.

Princess Diana at home in the gardens of Highgrove House in Tetbury, England. The Queen, Diana, and Charles at a royal engagement.

I was bleeding, and Charles just ignored me. He yelled at me, "Stop crying wolf!" Another time I was dashing about while holding a knife.

Dr. Dawson: Why were you cutting yourself and threatening suicide?

Princess Diana: I wanted attention because I was suffering from anguish, distress, and emotional pain. I was desperately crying out for help. Charles just slammed the door and rode off on his polo pony. Charles and the Queen blamed our marriage problems on my bulimia and my crazy behavior related to that.

The photo shows an earlier birthday of the Queen Mum with some of the royal family, including a very young Prince Harry and Princess Diana.

Dr. Dawson: Did the bulimia catch up to you? Any residual problems?

Princess Diana: On a trip to Canada I fainted while we were touring some exhibitions. Some royal aides took me to a room to recover. It was the result of exhaustion and not holding food down. I'd eat but vomit it up from the bulimic cycle. I was crying, weepy, and sobbing back at the hotel room in Vancouver.

Dr. Dawson: How did that Canadian trip come out?

By the time the Royal Couple visited South Korea in 1992, they could hardly stand each other. In 1992 they separated.

Princess Diana: I needed to get a lot of sleep, eat, and hold something down. But Charles was furious. He demanded that I go to functions that night because he said I was causing drama for him to explain.

A doctor saw me and gave me some pills. Charles had triggered the bulimia by telling me I was fat and then going to bed with Camilla. But I was too naïve and immature to articulate the problem at that time.

On December 9th, 1992, British Prime Minister John Major announced the formal separation of Prince Charles and Princess Diana.

Dr. Dawson: What was the point of the bulimic choice?

Princess Diana: I was able to lose weight. My waist went from 29 inches to 23 inches on the day of our marriage. But the price was not worth it to release tension by eating and vomiting. I was getting so sick and thin.

Dr. Dawson: Was the crazy behavior worth it?

Lady Hicks said his marriage to Princess Diana "absolutely destroyed" Prince Charles. Poor Charles could recover in Camilla's arms.

Princess Diana: I was aiming to get Charles' attention. But it backfired. I threw myself down the staircase and was just dismissed as a nut. I cut my wrists at times. I broke glass and threw things out the window. Again he told me, "Bloody, stop crying wolf."

Dr. Dawson: How did people take your irrational behavior?

Princess Diana: Everybody was scared about what I'd try next. I wasn't sleeping. I'd eat a lot but not gain weight because I vomited it all up.

Dr. Dawson: If you never ate, how did you survive?

James Hewitt and Victoria Silvstedt (left) at a TV press launch at the Soho Hotel in 2005. Grand Theft Parsons Premiere Party at Fred Whaur Harley Davidson Motorbike Shop in the Kings Road Chelsea in 2004 – Hewitt and an attractive lady (right). It seems Princess Diana's former lover has managed to struggle on in life.

Princess Diana: I always ate breakfast and kept it down. I was exercising by swimming and had enough energy. I went to bed early when I had some upcoming social engagement.

Dr. Dawson: But you somehow did your duty in public?

James Hewitt   Prince Harry   Prince Charles

Former soldier and playboy James Hewitt, 54, has been seen teaching Annie Cooper, 28, to play golf in Spain. Hewitt gave riding lessons to young Prince William and Prince Harry while having a sex affair with Princess Diana. Prince Harry (right) seemed to resemble Hewitt more than Prince Charles.

Princess Diana: Charles was very jealous of the attention and reaction I got from the public. My public role was to be this mythical, fairy-tale princess who would magically make everybody feel wonderful.

One appearance or touch from the Princess of Wales, and they'd have an enchanting, breathtaking, and captivating time. But in private, I was a horrible, crazy mess. I felt less than and not a part of the royal crowd.

Pictured are Princess Diana and her ex-lover James Hewitt. He offered to give her horsemanship tips and riding lessons. From there, sex and "love" developed.

Dr. Dawson: Did you get credit for the positive force you were presenting for the monarchy?

Princess Diana: No. I got criticism from Charles, who was jealous of the positive affection I got from the public. Charles had gone back to Camilla. He dismissed and ignored me at every opportunity.

Dr. Dawson: Any more critical incidents?

The Queen has long been said to have remained fond of her former daughter-in-law, but Prince Philip is said to be baffled by Fergie and Prince Andrew's relationship (left). Princess Diana (right) met James Hewitt as he was preparing for a military ritual as part of the wedding of Sarah and Prince Andrew. According to sources close to Hewitt, he claims in a documentary film that he and Diana had a reconciliation just seven months before her death. So he claims he wasn't a cad and a love rat.

Princess Diana: I got some therapy and was able to stop the bulimia. I learned to accept myself and raise my self-esteem. I used to think I was not good enough for Charles. I assumed I failed as a mother.

Dr. Dawson: How obvious were your symptoms?

Princess Diana: I was able to put on a happy front. At a party one time, I confronted Camilla and told her I knew what was going on between her and Charles. I was upset and cried later, but it felt good to express my feelings.

Pictured is the first day of the royal visit to Canada by Prince Charles and Diana, Princess of Wales, in June 1983. At times Diana, breathtakingly lovely and surprisingly thin, simply disappeared in the crowd. Secretly she was battling an eating disorder.

Charles told people we had a dreadful marriage because I was always sick, cracked, daft, and a crazy basket case. He didn't reveal the truth. A therapist once said to me that what other people think of me is none of my business. I've gotten into some spiritual concepts.

Dr. Dawson: That's right. Draw a line around yourself. Anything outside the circle is none of your business. According to my notes: In December 1992, Buckingham Palace announced your separation – the separation of the Prince and Princess of Wales.

Left: James Hewitt receives a trophy from Princess Diana. Right: Hewitt.

Princess Diana: Hopefully, I'll follow-up on the separation with a final divorce this year.

Dr. Dawson: In 1994, Charles confessed to adultery publicly on a TV documentary, and the details came out about the affair with Camilla Parker-Bowles and Charles, which began in 1972 in a 1994 book. It said Charles married you to please his father.

Princess Diana: After over 20 years, it is about time to admit it.

Dr. Dawson: Also, in 1994, another book came out which described an affair between you and Capt. James Hewitt from 1986 to 1991. In November 1995, you admitted in an interview that you were unfaithful to your husband with Hewitt. What was your relationship with Hewitt like, and how did that start?

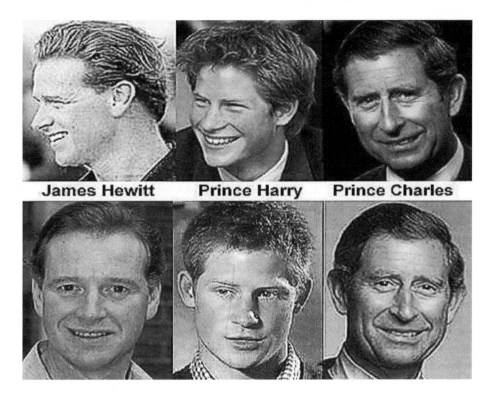

Jokes circulated because Hewitt resembled Prince Harry. But Prince Charles was Harry's father.

Princess Diana: Captain James Hewitt was teaching my boys horsemanship. He was a polo player who also helped show me riding skills.

Because Charles did not care for me and was inattentive to my needs, I was looking for some male companionship. Hewitt was charming, amusing, and sympathetic enough that a romantic relationship happened.

Dr. Dawson: You're quoted as saying, "I have lain awake at night loving you desperately and thanking God for bringing you into my life," in August 1989. Can you detail this five-year secret affair?

Harry was bonding with Hewitt, Diana's former lover. Harry got riding lessons from Hewitt.

Princess Diana: I met James Hewitt at a cocktail party in the fall of 1986 when I was 26, and he was 28. For some mysterious reason, neither the Palace nor Scotland Yard tried to stop Hewitt from seeing me.

Sometimes I wonder if Charles had set up the affair to combat rumors about Camilla.

Dr. Dawson: Hewitt wrote in his book on the affair, "Only one thing went wrong...We fell in love." Would you agree with that?

Diana's crazy love life resulted in tabloid press headlines.

Princess Diana: Many things unraveled in the affair with Hewitt. One problem was that he let his little-dick head think for his big head. His brains were in his trousers.

Dr. Dawson: I take it you were not having sex with your husband at the time of the Hewitt affair?

Princess Diana: Right. To the public, Charles and I were this glamorous royal couple with some kind of charisma and sex appeal according to the tabloids. In private, we were alienated, and Charles was loving Camilla.

Princess Diana sometimes wore sexy dresses which may have fueled her sex fantasy image for men.

I was supposed to be a sex fantasy to a lot of men. In reality, I slept alone and had no sex. Behind the dazzling, glitzy, enchanting veneer, my life was in ruin, shattered, and demolished by Charles. There were limits to propping up my self-esteem in therapy.

Dr. Dawson: From my notes, at the start of your affair, Hewitt described you as, "Emotionally very fragile...The bulimia had taken its toll on her..."

Diana suffered from eating disorders like bulimia. So she, at times, was very thin. She overcame the excessively skinny look by picking her clothing carefully.

"She was painfully thin, and her skin hung almost lifelessly on her bones. She was a woman deeply damaged by rejection." Was that correct?

Princess Diana: Oh my god! I sound like a bloody Nazi concentration camp prisoner. But I guess he had to come up with dramatic touches to sugarcoat his tell-all book on our sex affair.

Dr. Dawson: From what I researched, you set up meeting him. Right?

Princess Diana: He ran into me in the Palace, where he was attending some meetings on military ceremonies at the Palace for Sarah Ferguson and Prince Andrew's wedding in July.

He stared at me, and I said, "I like your Guards' uniform." I invited him to a cocktail party through my lady-in-waiting. At the party, he offered to give me some personal horseback instruction. One thing led to another.

9

Princess Diana had a talent for staying popular with the public. She was written-up and depicted in the media as a globetrotting humanitarian. Diana went on an Angola landmines walk to protest against mines. Prince Harry retraced her steps in Angola to continue the cause.

There were many pictures and videos of Diana on humanitarian missions advocating for unfortunate people who might be homeless alcoholics, drug addicts, or have various types of medical issues.

She cradled young children who were sick in various ways. And when she admitted having eating disorders, suicidal or self-mutilating cutting behavior, the public loved her as a sympathetic victim even more.

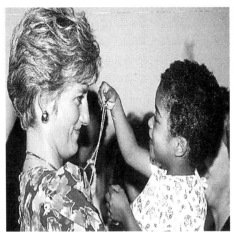

Left: Princess Diana got media attention doing humanitarian work, such as advocating for the sick or unfortunate. Right: Diana's anti-landmine campaign. Prince Harry retraced her steps, protesting landmines in Angola.

Because of Princess Diana's positive press, she got away with a lot of negative behavior. For example, after Oliver Hoare broke off his affair with Diana, she sexually harassed him by calling him 300 times. He was married at the time. If an average woman sexually harassed an ex-lover, she could have been arrested and charged with sexual harassment. But because of Diana's high status in the royal high orbit, she got away with it.

Diana developed resentment and got revenge from childhood into adulthood. She admitted to putting pins on chairs to stick and injure nannies she didn't like. Or she might throw the belongings of a nanny out the window when it was raining. The nanny would find her items stuck in the mud outside. When Prince Charles or other men she was sexually involved with didn't act the way she wanted, Diana would get revenge one way or another.

Left: Diana wore a daring, low-cut revenge dress when Prince Charles admitted adultery with Camilla. Center: Queen Elizabeth. Right: Diana did a revenge TV interview attacking Prince Charles and the royals.

In a video interview, Diana complained about Queen Elizabeth. She said she asked for help with Prince Charles because he was cheating on her with Camilla. Diana said the Queen shrugged and said, "I don't know what you can do. Charles is hopeless."

Diana went on about how in childhood, she was told she was the stupid one, and her brother was smart. Princess Diana, despite her privileges, money, and aristocratic social status liked to expose herself as a likable and sympathetic victim.

She said that whenever she did something right, she was never given any credit. "But if I tripped up, which I invariably did because I was new at the game, a ton of bricks came down on me. I coped with it with lots of tears and dived into the bulimia to escape."

Left: Diana and Charles when they were engaged – they smiled for photographers. Right: Prince Charles and Diana became increasingly cold and distant toward each other after they were married – unresolved conflicts between them piled up.

Diana complained that in the first part of her marriage to Prince Charles, the media attention made it difficult for them both. Then Prince Charles decided they would venture out alone, do public appearances separately. She wanted the company, but he did not.

Diana's marriage to Charles suffered due to their incompatibility and extramarital affairs. The couple separated in 1992, soon after the breakdown of their relationship became public knowledge. The details of their marital difficulties became increasingly publicized, and the marriage ended in divorce in 1996.

Princess Diana recalled at school, she used to go to the headmistress crying and said, "I wish I weren't so stupid." I was always conscious of being told I was stupid. She tended to get into self-pity.

Left: Diana at boarding school. Right: Diana and her brother during school days.

Diana wasn't precisely an A+ student. She was educated at home till the age of 9, then went to boarding school, Riddlesworth Hall in Norfolk, England. From the age of 12, she attended the exclusive West Heath Girls School in Kent, where again, she was not the best student.

After she failed all of her O-Levels twice, Diana dropped out at the age of 16. Then she tried a finishing school, Institut Alpin Videmanette, in Rougemont, Switzerland. But she quit again, this time after a single term. She was haunted by school failures.

In an interview, Diana pointed out that her depression, during her marriage to Charles, gave everybody a new label to show she was unstable.

Diana was a beautiful young teenage girl.

"And Diana is mentally unbalanced," Diana said. "And unfortunately that seems to have stuck. People used the label, and it stuck. When no one listens to you, all sorts of things start to happen. For instance, you have so much pain inside yourself that you try to hurt yourself on the outside because you want help."

"But it is the wrong help. You see, people then say you're crying wolf. People see it as crying wolf or attention-seeking. They think that because you're in the media all the time, you've got enough attention. But I was crying out because I wanted to get better."

"I wanted to go forward as wife, mother, Princess of Wales. So I did inflict conflicts on myself. I didn't like myself. I was ashamed that I couldn't cope with the pressures."

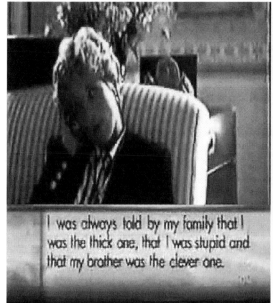

I was always told by my family that I was the thick one, that I was stupid and that my brother was the clever one.

Princess Diana was doing TV/video interviews.

"Well, I just hurt my arms and my legs. I work in environments now where I see women doing similar things. And I'm able to understand where they're coming from completely. I didn't always injure myself in front of Prince Charles."

"But anyone who loves someone would be very concerned about it. Charles didn't understand what was behind the physical act of hurting myself. But not many people would have taken the time to see that."

"I felt compelled to perform as the Princess of Wales. I wanted to do my engagements and not let people down. And support them and love them. And by being out in public, they were supporting me. Although they were not aware of just how much healing they were giving me and it carried me through."

Table 1

DSM-IV Diagnostic Criteria
Must meet five or more of the following:
Uses extreme measures to avoid real or imagined abandonment
Volatile relationships with others that can alternate between admiration and depreciation
Identity issues with an unstable self-esteem
Irresponsibility in at least two potentially harmful areas (e.g., spending, sex, substance abuse, reckless driving, binge eating)
Suicidal behavior, gestures, or threats
Self-mutilating behavior
Mood fluctuation with noticeable rapid changes
Persistent feelings of emptiness
Inappropriate, extreme, or hard to control anger
Short-lasting, stress-related paranoia or severe dissociation

DSM-IV: Diagnostic and Statistical Manual of Mental Disorders, 4th ed. Source: Reference 1.

Affective Dysregulation	
Frequent mood changes	Depressive "mood crashes"
Sensitivity to rejection	Outbursts of temper
Inappropriate intense anger	Anxiety
Uncontrolled anger	

Impulsive-Behavioral Dyscontrol	
Impulsive or spontaneous	Self-damaging behavior
Aggressive	(e.g., spending, sex,
Self-mutilation	substance abuse)

Cognitive-Perceptual Symptoms	
Suspicion	Derealization
Paranoia	Loss of identity
Illusions	Hallucination-like symptoms

"I felt I had to maintain the public image of a successful Princess of Wales. I had bulimia for several years. And that's like a secret disease. You inflict it upon yourself because your self-esteem is at a low ebb. And you don't think you're worthy or valuable."

Borderline Personality Disorder (**BPD**) is a mental disorder characterized by ongoing instability in mood, emotions, behavior, and perception of self-image. BPD is very frequently comorbid with other disorders, including anorexia, bulimia, anxiety, depression, self-harm, and more. The two charts above list the various characteristics involved in BPD.

Princess Diana had bulimia. Bulimia is an emotional disorder involving distortion of body image and an obsessive desire to lose weight, in which bouts of extreme overeating are followed by depression and self-induced vomiting, purging, or fasting.

The DSM (Diagnostic & Statistical Manual of the APA – American Psychiatric Association) criteria note that people with BPD have a pattern of symptoms and signs such as unstable relationships, unstable self-image, and mood swings, as well as impulsive behavior. These typically begin in early adulthood. To diagnose BPD, at least five of the following signs and symptoms must be present – Diana seemed to show most of these signs and symptoms of BPD:

1) Intense fears of abandonment

2) A pattern of unstable relationships

3) Unstable self-image

4) Impulsive and self-destructive behaviors

5) Suicidal behavior or self-injury

6) Wide mood swings

7) Chronic feelings of emptiness

8) Inappropriate anger

9) Periods of paranoia and loss of contact with reality

As you read the chapters I've included revealing psychotherapy sessions between myself and Princess Diana, you will find examples – at least in the subtext – of Diana's BPD characteristics.

10

Princess Diana unintentionally revealed her fundamental problem, which had blocked her recovery – picking the wrong men as her lovers. The focus in this chapter is on one of these men, Captain James Hewitt, who was involved with Princess Diana for about five years. Her romance with Hewitt revitalized Diana with new confidence and physical health.

However, she had a fatal flaw in picking men who, while handsome, were all headed in a different direction than she was. In the heat of sex and romance, lust overcame logic. But in the end, Diana and her lovers followed their life forces and agendas, which resulted in inevitable splits and a broken-hearted Princess Diana.

Dr. Dawson: Captain Hewitt reported you came on to him with the following quote, "I need you. You give me strength. I can't stand it when I'm away from you. I want to be with you. I've come to love you." Are those your words?

Major James Hewitt (left): Diana told him of the threats to her life and how Barry Mannakee had been "murdered". James Hewitt and Celia Walden (right) pictured in Marbella. The comeback cad?

Princess Diana: Yes, that sounds like me. When I get some romantic feelings, sometimes I like to stimulate the tempo. When I was in my teens and early 20s, I was very embarrassed, withdrawn, timid, and coy about expressing any kind of tenderness, affection, or passion.

After years of sleeping alone while married to Charles and crying my eyes out, I turned a corner and became more self-assured about romance. When Charles was away, I got sexually involved with Hewitt at Kensington Palace and Highgrove.

Jokes have been told about how Prince Harry resembles James Hewitt – was his biological father Prince Charles or Hewitt?

Dr. Dawson: How did you avoid this blowing up into a nasty sex scandal?

Princess Diana: That was slightly thorny, complicated, and risky. Captain Hewitt was quite skilled in the polo ponies. It made some sense to hire him to give my boys riding lessons. But it was a stretch and not plausible to some cynics, in my opinion.

To cover me further, I made it into a group social event and invited some friends as spectators to see the boys improve their horse-riding abilities while Hewitt gave them pointers.

It was reported that Princess Diana's interview with Martin Bashir made a shocked Prince Harry ask questions about his family. Princess Diana said he was aware of her lovers.

Dr. Dawson: How did it work?

Princess Diana: Hiding an affair when I am the Princess of Wales under intense press scrutiny – not to mention the focus from the monarchy – is a losing game over time. I knew eventually I'd be exposed.

I got obsessive-compulsive about it to the point of messing up the sheets on Captain Hewitt's bed to make it look like he slept there in case the maids noticed. There was a tendency of servants and assistants to gossip, which opened up these mini-scandals.

Pictured is James Hewitt at a polo match (left). Just about everyone denounced retired Maj. James Hewitt, whose claims of a royal romance were related in his book (*Princess in Love*), as a scoundrel. James Hewitt and Rebecca Loos Challenge TV Celebrity Poker Club in London (right).

Dr. Dawson: Did Prince Charles know about the Hewitt affair?

Princess Diana: Charles was aware I was sexually involved with Hewitt. We came to an understanding that he had Camilla Parker-Bowles, and I'd have my lovers from time to time.

Anyway, with our staff, police, and security systems monitoring my every move, any encounter, rendezvous, or assignation would get reported back to the royal family sooner or later.

Diana's ex-lover James Hewitt embarked on a new life in Spain. Hewitt and Carretera Cadiz-Barcelona partied at the Polo House, Marbella, Spain. Charles and Diana were relative newlyweds when this polo-match shot was taken (right).

Dr. Dawson: Your former personal protection officer commented on your love encounter with Hewitt: "He was a protest fuck." Was that what it was? Were you getting revenge by getting into sex trysts with Hewitt?

Princess Diana: No. If I wanted revenge, I would have jumped into sex affairs years earlier. Charles had abandoned me for Camilla, and God knows for who else from the start of our marriage. I was incredibly lonely and sex-starved. I'm human.

Princess Diana kept up a public image of being part of a happy family for years (left). Then the media revealed stories about her lovers (right).

Dr. Dawson: What was the perception of your sex and romantic life?

Princess Diana: Everybody assumed that I was having a fabulous life because they'd seen glamorized photos of me in magazines and newspapers. Behind the surface charm and glitziness, I was isolated, sexually deserted, and lonesome. Rip the façade of beautiful Princess Diana away, and you'd find I was just emotional rubble, sexual ruins, and loveless wreckage.

 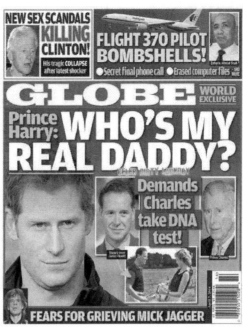

Tabloid newspapers had fun asking if Hewitt was Prince Harry's father.

Dr. Dawson: I read a quote from Hewitt, which showed that he was sort of patting himself on the back for straightening you out. He was on his way to Germany to his military unit. Here's what he said:

"In her bikini that afternoon, her skin fresh and tanned, her body in athletic shape thanks to her diet and her workouts, her expression so full of joy and free of worries, I reflected that she had come a long way – *we* had come a long way – from the bulimic girl I first encountered." Is that how you saw it?

Princess Diana: At the time, I was feeling somewhat abandoned and rejected by Hewitt since he was going to be stationed in Germany.

Diana's Hewitt romance led to her trying new things and having more confidence, such as riding (left). While Diana claimed she tried shooting, I could not find photos of her with a gun. However, I did find Kate Middleton (right) with a shotgun. Maybe it was a sign that Prince William and Kate were on the path to marriage when they were pictured together at Balmoral in matching Barbours walking and hunting.

I'm still not sure what was behind his transfer. After 4 or 5 years, I'd changed and developed. But imagine where I'd be if Charles had been a loving husband.

Dr. Dawson: What credit do you give him for your recovery?

Pictured are Princess Diana (left) on a hunting trip with Charles. She did not carry a shotgun. Camilla was an aggressive horsewoman (center) and Prince Charles (right) playing polo at Cirencester. Was this a hint that Camilla was more compatible with Prince Charles who was into polo and hunting?

Princess Diana: It should have been on the front page of every paper. Captain Hewitt, the soldier, rescues society girl from skeletal, gaunt, and emaciated bulimic hell like the Allies dragging Nazi-concentration-camp survivors to freedom.

The Queen should have presided over a special investiture for Captain Hewitt and bestowed upon him the Victoria Cross, the highest military decoration for valor in the battle of the sexes.

Dr. Dawson: From what I understand, your boys enjoyed Hewitt's company.

Princess Diana, Prince Harry, and James Hewitt. Hewitt later made money from their sex/love affair, wrote a book, and made media appearances such as on the Larry King TV show.

Princess Diana: He showed them around Windsor Barracks, had little military outfits made for them, and played with them on the Highgrove lawn. He had a black Labrador, and his dog used to tear up Charles' newly-planted gardens.

When the Prince of Wales rolled out of bed with Camilla and stopped in at Highgrove, he was furious about the damage to his prized new plantings. I thought he was going to have a heart attack.

Dr. Dawson: Any other benefits from the Hewitt romance?

After Princess Diana dumped James Hewitt, she went on to a series of lovers (left). But Hewitt claimed he still had feelings for her after her death and said, "Diana was dead. I wandered around in a state of shock. And then I cried." Hewitt got a lot of media attention in connection with Diana (right).

Princess Diana: After I was sexually satisfied, had some orgasms, and romantic relief, I was in the mood to do some of the usual country activities. Charles was the only one going on country walks before the Hewitt interlude.

Hewitt got me into taking country walks around the estate and becoming more confident on a horse. He encouraged me to get through some of my fears and try various things. Captain Hewitt got me into shooting and exploring country hobbies and recreations.

Being Princess Diana's ex-lover helped raise playboy James Hewitt's stud factor and attraction to women. James Hewitt and Michelle Collins in 2004 (right).

Dr. Dawson: How was Hewitt as a lover?

Princess Diana: He was a tall, good looking man with a lot of sex experience. And after five years, I was sexually more confident.

From Diana, the shy, fearful, and reluctant virgin, who married Charles, I became a poised, assertive, self-possessed, and secure lover. I even mastered the oral arts of sex. I think you Americans call it the blow job.

Dr. Dawson: I understand you even got slightly brazen and reckless in appearing with James Hewitt in public at a polo match? I saw a photo of you presenting an award to Hewitt.

Pictured are Alison Bell and James Hewitt (left). James Hewitt and Baroness Thyssen attended the opening of the Polo House (right). It appeared Hewitt liked royal or titled women.

Princess Diana: I was an honorary colonel-in-chief of the 13/18 Hussars' polo team. Hewitt was captain of the Life Guards' polo team. James was playing in the Inter-Regimental Championship at the Tidworth Polo Club in Hampshire.

Dr. Dawson: What did you do?

Princess Diana: I called the Hussars' commanding officer and told him I was attending. They let me award the prize, which was the Captains and Subalterns Trophy.

James Hewitt arrived at the home of his sister at Gidleigh Park near Chagford in Devon, England, Sunday, August 29, 1999. James liked to drive expensive sports cars and hang out with sexy women.

Dr. Dawson: What did you do that was so brazen and assertive?

Princess Diana: I betrayed my side by sitting with Hewitt, his mother, and his two sisters for a picnic. Hewitt was embarrassed and asked me why I wasn't with my polo team. I told my polo team I was just going to give the opposition a bit of encouragement.

Dr. Dawson: How'd it come out?

James Hewitt at his Polo House Club in Marbella (left). Hewitt liked rubbing shoulders with blue-blood nobles and upper-class royals he met playing polo, which irritated other soldiers. He had a reputation as being pretentious and an egomaniac. Hewitt is playing polo (right).

Princess Diana: I presented the trophy to the winning team, which happened to be the Life Guards, and Hewitt accepted the award from me. The photo was in all the papers. I was in a good mood.

Dr. Dawson: What happened to the eating disorder, self-injury, depression, and mood swings?

Princess Diana: There were points when I was confident and relatively healthy. I had distanced myself from the internal pain that caused me to hurt myself, throw myself downstairs, cut myself, and blubber my eyes out.

Diana wore a "Tomboy" outfit (left). Her humanitarian work included banning mines (right).

A few years ago, I got over the rampant bulimia. At least from the Hewitt affair, I got away from feeling no good at anything. But when I visited the dark side, I felt useless, hopeless, and a total failure at life.

Dr. Dawson: When Hewitt's book about your love affair with him was published, some people were afraid you might commit suicide.

Princess Diana: Well, I was in a grueling, grim, and demanding period at that time. But in tough times, I can always put on a happy front – I'm a good actress.

Pictured is Lady Diana Spencer fishing at Balmoral (left). Prince Charles and Princess Diana went to the family's Balmoral estate in Scotland after their wedding (right).

I've had former friends and ex-lovers sell me out before. What did Hewitt do wrong? He betrayed me, I'm not surprised, and I dumped him after five years.

Dr. Dawson: What was Hewitt's background?

Princess Diana: James Hewitt was raised in Kent, his father was a middle-class Marine officer, his mother was a housewife, and he has two sisters. It was a financial struggle, but his parents sent him to what Americans call an expensive private or prep school – Millfield. A Sandhurst graduate, he joined the Life Guards in 1978. He was socially ambitious.

The fact that Prince Charles preferred the company of Camilla showed that personality and compatible interests were vital in a love affair or marriage.

Dr. Dawson: How was he a social climber except for his affair with you?

Princess Diana: I got some feedback from his military colleagues who found him obsessed with money and power. It was like that American saying, a champagne appetite with a beer budget. He was charming, but he was conflicted about living beyond his means. He only made $48,000 in U.S. dollars, and yet he drove a $30,000 sports car.

James Hewitt went back home to Exeter in Devon, living with his mother. Princess Diana and James, at times, had their sex affair at his mother's place.

Dr. Dawson: What else did you learn about him?

Princess Diana: His fellow soldiers were aggravated because Hewitt was pretentious. He affected an aristocratic accent and demeanor.

James further irritated his fellow guardsmen by using his horsemanship skills to associate with blue blood, noblemen, and aristocrats on the polo field. Then he'd put on all sorts of airs and graces which didn't reflect the real, middle-class Hewitt.

Althorp House & Princess Diana: Diana and Hewitt sometimes made love at Althorp House. No tragic elements were showed, just facts of a fairytale-life she never lived. One of the rooms was filled with portraits of Diana's ancestors and family.

Dr. Dawson: He was a playboy?

Princess Diana: I got some dirt on Hewitt as far as the ladies went. He was very assertive, particularly when he spotted a pretty blonde.

Besides being a sucker for blondes, he's bragged that he bedded over 50 women in six-years.

Dr. Dawson: What happened to him after you two broke up?

Princess Diana: He next got involved with a TV weather girl, which caused her husband to divorce her.

Princess Diana and James Hewitt used Althorp House, at times, for their sex/love affair.

Dr. Dawson: From Hewitt's viewpoint, you became lovers in 1986 after that cocktail party. He claims you met with him at Windsor's Combermere Barracks, where you unloaded your troubles on him.

Princess Diana: He pumped me for information. I shared with him I was estranged from Charles. I had weekly riding lessons with him. I was lonely at the time.

My marriage had shattered like so many shards of broken glass and emotional debris. It was torture to live with Charles while he was busy having sex with Camilla. At times Charles would spend 30 nights or more consecutively in Camilla's bed.

James Hewitt: Ex-Life Guards officer James Hewitt was posted to Germany in 1989 and was later sent to fight in the Gulf War. Princess Diana was a sucker for a good-looking guy in a military uniform.

Dr. Dawson: What was Hewitt's response?

Princess Diana: I'm told his book reported that I was crying for help in the Palace wilderness like the spectral, eerie cry of an injured wild animal. Something like that. His co-writer helped with the analogies.

Sympathetically he told me, "You are not alone. You have me." Little did I know what it would cost me later.

Dr. Dawson: But you were madly in love with Captain Hewitt, right?

Pictured is James Hewitt fighting in the Gulf War.

Princess Diana: I'm positive that's the kind of thing he bragged about in his book.

Dr. Dawson: He claimed he was a selfless friend and an adventurous lover. He claimed you were hopelessly smitten with him.

Princess Diana: I was very lonely at that time, and he took advantage of that. I wouldn't call writing a tell-all-about-the-dirty-sex book precisely selfless. He got well paid.

Camilla Parker-Bowles entertained Prince Charles while Diana had her lovers on the side. Camilla played her cards right and ended up in a royal-love story.

Dr. Dawson: He revealed you two spun fantasies of marriage?

Princess Diana: Oh, you know how love affairs go. In the heat of passion, one says romantic things. There were moments when we were in sync while lying by the swimming pool at Highgrove. Passionate comments can get twisted in meaning. Or cuddle with a lover in bed where starry-eyed, dreamy remarks are exchanged.

Dr. Dawson: He said you had hot, sexy trysts at Althorp, a bathroom at Highgrove, and his mother's modest place in Ebford, Devon.

In addition to the sex all over the place, Hewitt claims he researched bulimia and made healthy suggestions for you.

Princess Diana: He advised me to keep down healthy meals to combat bulimia. But that's just common sense. Did I need amazing, "Diet-Professor" Hewitt to figure that out?

Dr. Dawson: From what I've read, you bought some expensive items for him?

Princess Diana: As was recorded in that well-known Gilbey phone call, I spoke about buying things for Hewitt. I dressed him entirely from head to foot. It cost me a lot.

I gave him expensive shirts, Savile Row suits, and a diamond-studded tie pin. He enjoyed impressing people by showing off his expensive clothing and items I bought him.

Dr. Dawson: When he was transferred to Germany and sent to the Persian Gulf with a tank company in 1991, you'd cooled off your feelings for him. Right?

Princess Diana: I was concerned when he was in the Persian Gulf conflict. He was battling the Iraqi army with his men.

Dr. Dawson: He claims you wrote him a lot of adoring love letters which were signed "Dibbs" – your nickname. And that these letters proved the love affair and helped him sell the book to a co-writer and publisher. It was concluded that the relationship was "too beautiful" to keep secret.

Princess Diana: I've learned the hard way to be very careful about what I put in writing. Because it often came back to haunt me.

Dr. Dawson: It was reported that you were frantic for news of the Persian Gulf War, you were very anxious, and had many sleepless nights worrying about Hewitt's safety.

Princess Diana: To sell their books, the authors exaggerate and portray me as a pathetic puddle of overheated female hormones. Hewitt got a ghostwriter to embellish and dramatize the book with sexy romantic flourishes. Romance novels sell well to women in particular. His book hype sounds like those bodice-ripper novels.

Dr. Dawson: You became the star of his erotically over-charged tale of a tragically doomed love affair between a royal princess and her lover - a dashing, polo-playing military officer.

Princess Diana: Those romantic novels are one of my guilty pleasures. They're full of those cheesy, passionate, and clichéd lines like "she squealed with a lust for love, she trembled with desire, and he thrust into her with craving." Very spectacular.

11

Diana discussed her childhood memories in this chapter. The divorce of her parents impacted her and her brother in particular. Most of the time, her older sisters were away at boarding school. Her mother and stepfather spoiled her, and her brother rotten.

She learned some gratitude and discipline from her father, who demanded that Diana and her brother write thank-you notes to those who gave them gifts or invited them to parties and social functions.

As a child, Diana was threatened by the pretty, sexy, and young nannies her father would hire. She did not want them to take her mother's place. Diana and her brother would terrorize the nannies with mean pranks.

Left: Diana as a toddler. Center: Kate Middleton, early childhood. Right: Meghan Markle, toddler stage, with her mother and father.

Dr. Dawson: Okay, let's put the boyfriends on the back burner for now and focus on your childhood. Tell me what you recall about your childhood. You were born July 1st, 1961, named Diana Frances Spencer - born to Frances and Edward John (Johnnie) Spencer. Your father later becomes the 8th Earl Spencer.

Princess Diana: I was not born in a hospital; I was born at home. My parents' marriage was dysfunctional; they split. My Mummy left our home, and my brother and sisters lived with Daddy.

Left: Diana as a young child. Center: Kate Middleton, young child. Right: Meghan Markle in childhood and her mother.

Dr. Dawson: How did you adapt to the chaos and dysfunction set off by your parents' divorce?

Princess Diana: We were off at boarding schools and at the time in childhood we didn't know any better. My brother claimed that the divorce had a tremendous impact on him after he grew up and got married.

So my siblings' growth and development were mainly out of my sight and mind. I'd suddenly see them when they came back from school on vacation or whatever, and they'd changed.

Dr. Dawson: Maybe your parents' divorce and mismatch biased you unconsciously in your choice of men for a romantic relationship from Charles onward. What do you think?

Left: Diana and her brother Charles (Earl Spencer). Center: Meghan Markle and her half-sister Samantha. Right: Kate and sister Pippa Middleton, bridesmaids.

Princess Diana: I can only judge by the results, and I'd have to agree I've picked men poorly – always ending up with the wrong man who was not compatible over long periods.

Dr. Dawson: What was your relationship with your sisters and brother?

Princess Diana: Sarah is my oldest sister, and I looked up to her, idolized her. I did her favors to show my affection for her. I made her bed, ran her bath, packed her suitcase, and ran errands for her. I also helped out my brother a lot. But my sisters were quite liberated, independent, and self-reliant.

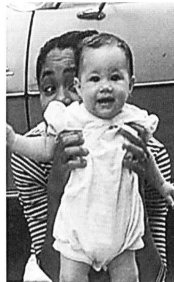

Left: Baby Diana. Center: Baby Meghan Markle and her mother. Right: Baby Kate Middleton and her mother.

Dr. Dawson: At home, who took care of you?

Princess Diana: Mostly, my brother and I were at home at the same time and looked after by various nannies. We played dirty tricks on them. I'm sorry in retrospect, particularly since I worked as a nanny in my late teens and felt the frustration when children rebel.

Dr. Dawson: You played dirty tricks and pranks on the nannies?

Princess Diana: Yes, one extraordinarily mean and hurtful prank was to stick pins in the cushions on their chairs. They'd sit down and scream in pain while pulling pins out of their butts.

It was her father, Earl of Spencer, who mostly brought up Diana. When he became the 8th Earl of Spencer, he moved the family to Althorp. Diana and her brother Charles (right).

Dr. Dawson: I hope you've made amends for that.

Princess Diana: I know. I'm humiliated now. Another dirty trick was to toss the nannies belongings, clothing, whatever out the window. When it was raining at night, it was a horror for the nanny to find their items. Soggy, muddy clothing tossed in the dirt in a garden, for example.

Dr. Dawson: Why were you and your brother so mean and such juvenile delinquents?

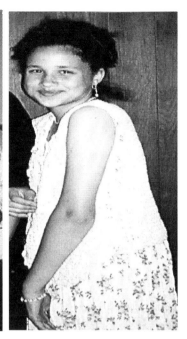

Left: Lady Diana, age 14.   Center: Teenage Kate Middleton. Right: Meghan Markle, teenager.

Princess Diana: As I recall now, we were furious because Mummy had left us. And Daddy was selecting these beautiful, young, and sexy nannies to care for us. I think he was sleeping with some of them.

Dr. Dawson: How did you feel about your father's possible sex life?

Princess Diana: We were traumatized because we'd return for vacation from school, and suddenly, we'd meet a new hot, young, shapely babe Daddy would call our nanny. We suspected they were his mistresses.

Left: Diana, 16, pictured in a chalet in Switzerland in 1977. Center: Meghan Markle, 15, in front of Buckingham Palace. Right: Kate Middleton, 17.

But we never caught him in bed with them. He'd take the nannies for long rides in the country in his car, and perhaps he had sexual intercourse at some hotel down the road.

Dr. Dawson: You were threatened because one of those nannies could become your new stepmother? Or your father's mistress?

Princess Diana: Mistress. Daddy would be looking for an upper-class, proper wife to replace Mummy.

Dr. Dawson: How did you feel about your childhood?

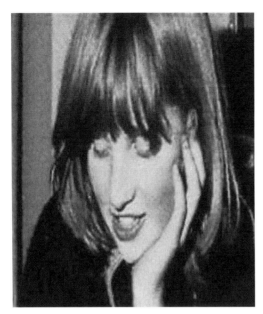 

Diana, as a young teenager (left). Lady Diana Spencer in her late-teens (right) is pictured.

Princess Diana: I felt like an outsider, isolated, and shut out of my parents' marital secrets. Daddy and Mummy were always fighting, and my mother often was crying. Neither Daddy nor Mummy spoke to us about their conflicts.

Dr. Dawson: How did your father handle it after your mother left?

Princess Diana: After my mother left, Daddy patched the family together with the series of sexy, young nannies. I wasn't comfortable asking Daddy or Mummy why they were fighting and splitting. So my childhood was miserable, isolating, and unhappy.

Following her parents' acrimonious divorce in 1969 (over Lady Althorp's affair with wallpaper heir Peter Shand Kydd), Diana was shocked (left). Peter and Frances Shand-Kydd with their daughter Lady Sarah (right).

Dr. Dawson: What did you talk to your father about in childhood?

Princess Diana: I remember telling him I might marry an ambassador when I was 13. I don't know why I wanted to marry somebody in public service. Probably because I was too naïve to expect the stress of having dozens of press members hounding me.

Dr. Dawson: How did you do in school?

Pictures of Princess Diana's parents on their wedding day at Westminster Abbey in 1954. They moved to Althorp when her father succeeded to the Earldom in 1975.

Princess Diana: I struggled in school. Perhaps I was bored. Maybe I just did not want to apply myself. I was failing the exams. My parents had wanted a boy, and they ended up with me, a girl. Eventually, I dropped out of school.

Dr. Dawson: What did you like?

Princess Diana: I enjoyed pets, even guinea pigs. I had a collection of stuffed animals I slept with. Sometimes at night, I'd hear Mummy crying, and then I'd start crying. My brother would join in sobbing in his bedroom, and I listened to him.

Diana's family without her mother. Diana at right.

Dr. Dawson: Wasn't that noisy?

Princess Diana: It was a whole concert of bawling, sniveling, and weeping. Mummy was depressed and wailing. Then I was sad and howling. And my brother joined in sniveling, crying, and shrieking. It was a horror movie soundtrack set in an insane asylum.

Dr. Dawson: What was it like after your parents separated and later divorced?

Princess Diana: Mummy would visit us sometimes, then she'd start to cry. I asked her why she was upset. She said she was sorry to leave us.

Pictured are Princess Diana talking With Raine, Countess Spencer, her stepmother. She had a troubled relationship with Raine. Princess Diana and her mother, Frances Shand Kydd, attended a wedding on September 16th, 1989.

Dr. Dawson: Did your parents compete for your affection or attention?

Princess Diana: Yes. They'd both give us presents, including clothing. Sometimes I was uncertain about which outfit to wear because I did not want to offend Daddy by wearing something Mummy gave me.

Conversely, if Daddy gave me something to wear and I put it on in Mummy's presence, I was self-conscious. I was crazy to be so sensitive.

Pictured is Earl Spencer and his first wife, Frances Shand Kydd, at the 1978 wedding of their daughter Lady Jane.

Dr. Dawson: Sounds like you were a people-pleaser starting in your childhood.

Princess Diana: Yes, I'm a pretty fair actress. I will try to act in such a way to please another. I have a high need for approval.

Dr. Dawson: How did the divorce go?

Princess Diana: Daddy was bent on blaming Mummy and keeping control of us children. I recall a warning at Riddlesworth – my prep school – that my father was sending a lawyer or judge to my school as part of some divorce proceeding.

Teenage Diana.

Dr. Dawson: How did you feel about the divorce?

Princess Diana: Because my parents were divorcing, I felt excluded from my peer group at school. Because few children's parents were divorced then, but after a few years, half the school's children were from broken homes. Divorce almost became stylish.

Dr. Dawson: Your mother remarried, right?

Left: Princess Diana, at right, stands with stepmother, Raine, Countess Spencer, and her sister. Right: Diana and her brother, Charles Spencer.

Princess Diana: Yes, my new stepfather – Peter Shand Kydd – was very nice to us. Too nice. Mummy and Peter tried to spoil us and were successful, making a fuss over us children and spoiling us rotten.

Dr. Dawson: Did the other children at school treat you differently since your parents were separated and divorced?

Princess Diana: Actually, it was getting pretty common to have divorced parents, stepmothers, stepfathers, and family tension among many students. The result was that at least I could identify with half the students at school with similar issues.

Dr. Dawson: Did your parents give you any tips in growing up?

Princess Diana: Strangely, Daddy urged me to be democratic and respectful to everybody.

Dr. Dawson: Why "strangely"?

Princess Diana: Daddy was an aristocrat, a nobleman. Sometimes the upper-class types are snobbish and disrespectful to those from modest, middle-class, or lower-class backgrounds.

But he told me always to treat people with respect, individually, and to be friendly. So I spoke to the average person – soldier, policeman, construction worker, grocery clerk, and so forth.

Dr. Dawson: What else did your parents teach you?

Princess Diana: Mummy and especially Daddy demanded that we were polite with people on holidays who had given us presents or invited us to dinners or social engagements.

Dr. Dawson: How did you show that?

Princess Diana: We had to write thank-you notes for gifts, to hosts of parties, or organizers of polo balls and other social functions. And we had to do it immediately. That became a habit with me. I'd write a thank-you note after attending a social engagement the same night.

Dr. Dawson: What else do you recall about childhood?

Princess Diana: Every year, we were dragged to the Queen's Norfolk residence – Sandringham – on the holidays. My brother and I hated it because it was boring. They'd show us the same movies over and over again. But Daddy forced us to go.

Dr. Dawson: Were you split between your parents on the holidays?

Princess Diana: Yes, two weeks with Daddy and two weeks with Mummy. We would have settled for a hug. But instead, we were bought off with material gifts. My older sisters escaped the holiday problem because they were away at boarding school.

12

Princess Diana recalled her boarding school experiences, revealed some minor difficulties at school, and reported on some critical incidents in this chapter. At 13, her family moved to Althorp, she had conflicts with her stepmother, and her father had a severe illness. She also remarked on raising William and Harry.

Dr. Dawson: Can you go back to your childhood? How did you do at boarding school?

Princess Diana: I was in the habit of looking after my father, and so I resisted being sent to Riddlesworth Hall, the prep school. I was a jolly bitch trying to blackmail Daddy emotionally.

I yelled at him that he didn't love me because he was leaving me at boarding school. I didn't want to go.

Left: Teenage Diana and her friend Lucy Coats in 1975. The pair loved listening to music together. Center: Kate Middleton (right) and her teen friends. Right: Teenage Meghan Markle and friends.

Dr. Dawson: Did it work?

Princess Diana: No. I had to go to boarding school. I enjoyed the Riddlesworth. I was a rebel and messed around too much, which alarmed school authorities. I joked around and broke school rules.

It was too boring just to sit quietly and learn dry material. It was fun to put on makeup and appear in school plays. I avoided taking speaking parts. The plots were silly, and the roles were unintentionally funny.

Over a year after her mother finally married Peter Shand-Kydd, Diana was sent to her first boarding school, Riddlesworth Hall, in Norfolk. Diana was not a particularly motivated student. She was educated at home till the age of 9, went to Riddlesworth Hall from age 9-12 (left). Diana, in 1977 (right). She finished her schooling in Kent at West Heath secondary school, while her father, Earl Spencer, married Raine, Countess of Dartmouth.

Dr. Dawson: Weren't you good at swimming?

Princess Diana: I won sporting cups – awards for swimming and diving. But in academic subjects, I did poorly. I just could not focus or get motivated to study boring material.

Dr. Dawson: How did your siblings do with academic material?

Diana (left) leaving for Riddlesworth Hall, near Diss in Norfolk, after holidays in 1972. It's a school with an exciting piece of history since Princess Diana was a pupil at Riddlesworth (center). Right: Kate Middleton at school (seated in the center).

Princess Diana: My brother, Charles, seemed to be the brains of the family. He was excellent in the classroom. My parents sent me to finishing school in Switzerland – the Institut Alpin Videmanette. I felt like a misfit there. I did learn to ski. It was costly, and I told my parents it was a waste of their money.

Dr. Dawson: Did you get into trouble at Riddlesworth Hall?

Princess Diana: One night, I was challenged and dared to go out to the school gate at 9:00 PM. A long walk to the gate. But where was the girl with the candy for me? I got there, and it was a joke because nobody showed up.

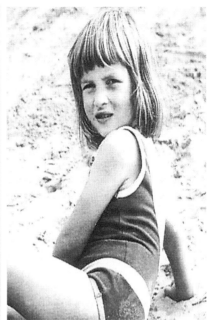

Until 1970, Diana was a pupil at Silfield Nursery School at King's Lynn, Norfolk, when she went to a girls' preparatory school, Riddlesworth Hall.

Dr. Dawson: What happened next?

Princess Diana: Suddenly, emergency police and ambulance vehicles raced through the gate. I hid from the police cars behind the gate. I was reported missing. Lights came on at the school in the distance.

Dr. Dawson: What did the school authorities do?

Princess Diana: The school called my parents, who were divorced. They both came. It turned out that some girl had set off an alarm because she said she had appendicitis, which was a false alarm.

  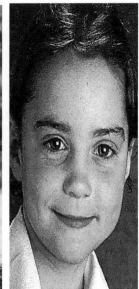 

Left to right: Diana Spencer, pictured is very young Diana at the beach and practicing ballet as a teenager. Kate Middleton childhood photo. Meghan Markle on a horse as a child.

I wandered back to my room an hour later. My parents took it well after I explained I was out walking to the gate on a dare. They were relieved and amused.

Dr. Dawson: How was your health at school?

Princess Diana: I was okay. Except for my eating disorder starting in that, I was over-eating. Some of the girls made fun of me and dared me to eat more. I'd eat extra kippers and bread at breakfast to amuse the girls.

Dr. Dawson: Any other habits?

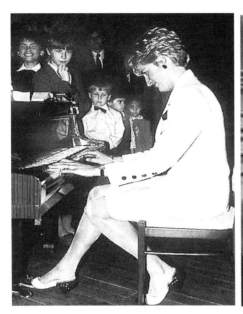

Princess Diana (left) played the piano to patients at a children's hospital in Prague, May 1991. Her piano lessons paid off. Diana learned to play the piano when she was a pupil at West Heath school (right).

Princess Diana: I'd dance ballet. The only way I could do it was to creep secretly down to this massive hall at night. For hours I'd dance ballet and listen to music. Then I'd tiptoe back upstairs to my room. I never got caught.

Dr. Dawson: What activities did you like?

Princess Diana: I loved playing the piano. Tap dancing was fun. Tennis was a favorite of mine. Because I was tall, I was captain of the netball team. I played hockey.

Left: Teenage Lady Diana Spencer and her brother Charles, Viscount Althorp. Althorp. Right: Kate and sister Pippa Middleton, teenagers, on a sports field.

I loved outdoor activities. I volunteered to visit older adults and those at a local mental hospital or asylum weekly. Perhaps it was setting me up for that sort of charity work. I enjoyed it.

Dr. Dawson: Did you date and have boyfriends?

Princess Diana: After a few years in school, all my girlfriends had boyfriends. But I didn't date or have a boyfriend. I guess I had an intuition that I should keep myself pure and tidy for something better in the future.

Although I made the mistake of trying to be friends with boys, my sisters had rejected, I admired the boys when they were my sisters' boyfriends. My sisters didn't like it.

Left: Princess Diana took William and Harry on a carriage ride. Right: Kate Middleton takes George and Charlotte to a London club.

Dr. Dawson: How did you get along with the other girls at school?

Princess Diana: I had many friends. I had a rebel tendency. But I understood how to behave when needed. At times I was very noisy and got into minor disruptions.

Dr. Dawson: What other critical incidents do you recall?

Princess Diana: We moved to Althorp in Northhampton when I was 13. It was traumatic for me because I had to leave behind all my friends from Norfolk. To add insult to injury, my stepmother, Raine, came on the scene.

Left: Prince Harry, Meghan Markle, and baby Archie. Right: Prince William and Kate Middleton, the future King and Queen consort of England, Prince George, Princess Charlotte, Prince Louis. Kate may be announcing her 4th pregnancy fairly soon.

My siblings and I hated her because she spent Daddy's money, decorated, and changed the house. Maybe I was too hard on her.

Dr. Dawson: How was your father doing?

Princess Diana: Another shock was when my father got sick. He had a brain hemorrhage. Daddy was having these bloody headaches, which he kept secret. Then suddenly, he collapsed. I went to see him in a London hospital. He was gravely ill.

Daddy's brain ruptured. While Raine blocked us from seeing him, my eldest sister went to see him, and he had a tracheotomy. So he couldn't talk. Fortunately, he recovered, but it changed him. He's been somewhat estranged.

Dr. Dawson: How did you raise William and Harry?

Princess Diana: I've heard that expression "William is an heir and Harry is a spare." I've tried to help them feel secure and loved. I've taught them not to expect or anticipate things – that way they, won't be disappointed. I've tried to follow that lesson myself.

I'd hug them and ask, "Who loves you the most in the world?" And they'd say, "Mummy." I've tried to coach William on navigating the monarchy. From his father and me, William has a pretty good idea about his responsibilities.

13

Diana shared her experiences in her love affair with Dr. Hasnat Khan. She appeared to suffer from low self-esteem and fears of abandonment, perhaps related to feeling abandoned by her mother as a child when her parents divorced.

Because she fit the BPD syndrome with symptoms of volatile interpersonal relationships, she had been unable to keep a stable romantic relationship with a man. She picked the wrong man over and over and maybe on an unconscious level knew she'd be rejected. She rationalized efforts to rescue a doomed love affair. Diana went to extremes to force relationships to work.

Dr. Dawson: Let's get back to your romantic conflicts with men. Why do you think you're not able to have a stable and happy romance leading to a solid marriage?

Left to right: Hasnat Khan, Diana. A film scene is depicting Princess Diana meeting Hasnat Khan in a hospital. Meghan Markle's ex-boyfriends.

Princess Diana: I don't know. My romances never work out. My love life is a jolly mess. I was speaking to a girlfriend of mine who has tried to help me be more practical.

She said, "You're picking the wrong men who are too different from you, have different goals, and won't fit into your lifestyle. Take, for example, Dr. Hasnat Khan. He's a Muslim from Pakistan. I've had friends in college who were Muslims from Pakistan."

"They always have a family or relatives back in Pakistan who insist that they marry a nice Muslim woman from Pakistan. Why are you going through the hassle and trouble of trying to overcome cultural, ethnic, and religious differences to find a husband the hard way?"

Left: At Marlborough College, Kate Middleton dated first love Willem Marx. Center: Kate and an old flame. Right: Kate and Prince William, 2005.

I told her, "When I fall in love, I don't calculate all that." What do you think, Doctor?

Dr. Dawson: As your psychotherapist and psychologist, I don't see it as my role to pick boyfriends for you.

Princess Diana: Some of my friends have told me, "It's not enough to have a couple of romantic variables like he's handsome, and he helps people in the medical field. How about the thousands of other variables working against you?"

Left: King Juan Carlos made a pass at Princess Diana. Right: A scene from *William and Kate*, a movie depicting their budding college romance.

But once I fall in love, I try to make it work. What do you think is going to happen?

Dr. Dawson: I think like any addiction, you'll continue to cycle through various lovers until you hit bottom. You've had unstable relationships from Prince Charles forward, and it will continue. But let's be positive and hope for the best.

Princess Diana: Victoria told me, "You can talk yourself into being in love with lots of different men. Romance with Hasnat Khan is doomed." What can I do to get to a stable relationship?

Princess Diana and Prince Charles appeared unhappy (left). Diana was "the People's Princess." Her tale was full of heartache, enemies, love, life, and of course, tragedy.

Dr. Dawson: To get to the goal of a stable love relationship, you'll need to continue intensive, long-term psychotherapy to help you balance your unconscious conflicts. Keep taking actions with men you're interested in romantically, and it will all work out eventually. Tell me about Dr. Hasnat Khan. How did you meet and how did the romance happen?

Princess Diana: I'd gone to the Royal Brompton Hospital with my acupuncturist-nurse friend whose husband was sick with a heart problem in the fall of 1995.

Left: Princess Diana with Dodi Fayed. Royal ex-girlfriends. Right: Prince Charles and Lady Sarah Spencer, Diana's older sister; Prince William and Olivia Hunt; Prince Harry and Chelsy Davy.

Dr. Hasnat Khan, who I started calling "The One," came to check up on her husband. He struck me as drop-dead gorgeous. Maybe because I'm blonde and he's dark. He took no notice of me, and I'm not used to being ignored.

Dr. Dawson: He was a challenge for you?

Princess Diana: Yes. I started visiting my friend's husband at the hospital as an excuse to meet Dr. Khan again. I read books on cardiology. I bought some Pakistani clothing – the silk tunic and trousers worn by Pakistani women.

Left: Two of Diana's lovers. The earliest of Diana's illicit loves was her bodyguard and confidant, Barry Mannakee (left). The married Mannakee worked at Kensington Palace for about a year. Oliver Hoare (right), an Islamic art dealer and a friend to Prince Charles, was said to have become close to Diana in 1992, after the death of her father. Right: Prince Harry and ex-flame Chelsy Davy.

I was considering converting to Islam. I watched him perform open-heart surgery. I ended up in bed with Hasnat Khan in his over-night hospital room.

Dr. Dawson: Where was the press in all this hot sex and romance?

Princess Diana: A photographer caught me entering the hospital after midnight. I threw them off by telling a reporter that I comfort terminally ill patients several nights a week for a few hours.

Left: Bodyguard Barry Mannakee and Princess Diana. Right: Cressida Bonas, Prince Harry's ex-girlfriend.

I said to the reporter, "I'm there for them... I draw strength from them. They need someone. I hold their hands, talk, whatever helps." Then the papers had headlines like "My Secret Nights as an Angel" and spread the story.

Dr. Dawson: What were you getting out of the romance with Hasnat?

Princess Diana: Well, for a time, I was at peace, and he was filling my needs. He was dedicated to his medical career and didn't want any money from me. I offered to buy him a car, and he turned me down. One problem was that he was terrified of publicity or reporters bothering him at the hospital.

Left: Oliver Hoare was one of Princess Diana's lovers. Right: Prince Harry, his ex-girlfriends, and rumored flings: Chelsy Davy, Cressida Bonas, Natalie Pinkham, Cassie Sumner, Catherine Ommanney, Caroline Flack.

Dr. Dawson: And part of the Princess of Wales package is plenty of publicity, reporters, photographers, and paparazzi.

Princess Diana: I'm stubborn in love.   One of my friends said, "Why are you so clueless when an incompatibility is obvious?   It's not spiritual to force things. You're showing your self-will running riot."

Dr. Dawson: Okay, what did you do with Dr. Khan to make it work?

Dodi Fayed (left). Diana didn't wait long to rebound after the breakup with Khan. A month later, she was dating Dodi Fayed. But the relationship didn't last long. Dodi was a cocaine addict who survived on a trust fund from his father. He sometimes produced movies in Hollywood. Diana's friendship with England rugby captain Will Carling (right) led to the end of his marriage.

Princess Diana: I set up a den for him in my apartment at Kensington Palace so he could drink beer and watch football. At his apartment, I made myself useful by cleaning, vacuuming, washed dishes, and ironed his shirts.

A girlfriend said, "Princess Diana turns herself inside out, makes herself over into a housewife or maid. How else did you knock yourself out trying to people-please Hasnat?" I was very talented at keeping my love life secret from the press.

Two of Princess Diana's lovers: Will Carling (left) and Oliver Hoare (right).

When Hasnat and I quarreled, my butler would leave a message for him at a pub he frequented near the hospital.

Dr. Dawson: Your friends are critical and say you're desperate?

Princess Diana: Desperate? I made trips to Pakistan with charity and humanitarian causes as my cover. I met with Jemima Khan, the daughter of Annabel and Jimmy Goldsmith. She had married a Pakistani cricket legend. We talked about how to handle marriage to a Muslim – how to overcome traditional objections to non-Pakistani women like me.

Princess Diana visited Pakistan (left) and met with her friend Jemima Khan, on a visit to young cancer patients at a hospital in Pakistan, 1997. This little-known English public relations executive, James Gilbey (right), was known to refer to Princess Diana as "Squidgy." Gilbey was one of Diana's lovers.

A girlfriend was sarcastic and asked, "She gave you the formula to trap Hasnat using desperate tactics?" But I got no such formula.

Dr. Dawson: What else did you try?

Princess Diana: I sent my butler to ask a priest if I could marry Hasnat without notifying the authorities. The Roman Catholic priest said it was not possible to marry without informing the religious authorities.

Dr. Dawson: How did Dr. Khan react?

Khan leaned into Princess Diana's BMW, near the Royal Brompton Hospital, London, 1996. With some success, Diana worked hard to keep the press away from Khan.

Princess Diana: He was furious and angrily yelled at me, "Do you think you can just have a priest stop off at my apartment and marry us? Are you crazy?"

A friend trying to help lectured me: "You were wondering why your lovers don't work out to be the man of your dreams and marry you? You're the most famous, beautiful, and desirable woman in the world. And you're acting like an infatuated, dreamy, dazed, irrational, confused, overemotional, soppy, infatuated, lovesick teenage girl chasing a guy who doesn't want to marry you."

Princess Diana is leaving the English National Ballet, London, 1996. Diana was on her cell phone aboard the *Jonikal,* near St. Tropez, after her relationship with Dodi Al Fayed, had begun. At least Dodi could take a date out on a yacht.

But it seemed like it could work! I was madly in love with him. Why couldn't I make it work?

My girlfriend was attacking me and said:

"You expected a Pakistani-Muslim doctor, who works overtime at a hospital, to forget his cultural and religious and family heritage and medical occupation, grab his doctor's bag, and join you as you travel saving the world?"

Princess Diana had broken off the relationship out of frustration that Hasnat wouldn't agree to marry or even to go public. Hasnat was a decent, intensely private man from a traditional, conservative Pakistani family, and he was worried about how it would work. Diana always went after men who presented an impossible challenge.

"You and Khan would be fighting landmines, curing AIDS, and focusing the press on various humanitarian causes. Then between rescue missions, you can party on a yacht with Dr. Khan, then attend fashion shows and charity balls with your new doctor husband. Right?"

Dr. Dawson: What else did you do in this romance?

Princess Diana: I took a trip with some friends to Lahore, Pakistan, to do fund-raising for the Shaukat Khanum Memorial Cancer Hospital. That was just a cover. I was aiming to get a lot of publicity to impress Hasnat Khan's family in Pakistan.

Princess Diana, center, with playboy Spain's King Juan Carlos, left, and Queen Sofia.

I was trying to show that I could be representing a severe health cause. That way, since Hasnat was a serious-minded heart surgeon, he'd be impressed along with his family.

A girlfriend yelled at me: "It's incredible to see the crazy extremes you will go to in trapping a husband. You've got your choice of almost any single man on Earth. And yet you chase after some guy you can't have!"

"There are thousands of other men you could get who would be better than Hasnat."

Kate Middleton wore a headscarf while touring in Malaysia that was similar to the one Princess Diana wore.

Dr. Dawson: Okay, how did this one-sided courtship race work out? What else did you do to chase Dr. Khan?

Princess Diana: In 1994, I gave out soup to starving, sick children in Zimbabwe. I was crusading to ban the use of land mines and hurry their clearance. Adding serious medical causes were logical. Hasnat would then see that I was earnest about medical problems just like he is.

Dr. Dawson: How did Hasnat respond?

Left: Hasnat Khan and his parents in Pakistan. Center: Diana and her father. Right: Diana and her mother.

Princess Diana: When news of our love affair hit the newspapers, Hasnat was distraught, and our relationship became stormy. I can see the headline: "Shy Di's New Man!"

Dr. Dawson: What did Dr. Khan do?

Princess Diana: He cut me off! Oh my god! I was hysterical.

Dr. Dawson: Then what happened?

Princess Diana: Hasnat was insanely afraid of going public. Friends told me he had no intention of marrying me. I told a reporter that the story about Hasnat and me in a romance was false.

"An English girl is every conservative Pashtun mother's worst nightmare," Jemima Khan advised. "You send your son to be educated in England, and he comes back with an English bride. It's something they dread." Jemima Khan revealed that Diana tried her hardest to fit in with Hasnat's family in Pakistan.

A girlfriend cross-examined me, "What did you find out about Hasnat's ethnic background and family? Because as you found out the hard way with the Windsors, when you marry a man, you marry his family."

Dr. Dawson: What did you find out?

Princess Diana: His family was Pathan, which is a group of people who originated between Pakistan and Afghanistan. The Pathan group of Muslims are passionate about their cultural, religious, and family traditions.

Princess Diana and Jemima Khan. Jemima gave Diana pointers on bridging the cultural gap in a romance with a Muslim man.

So they did not want me. I took that as a challenge. Hasnat told me that his parents had tried several times to marry him off to a proper Pathan Pakistani Muslim bride.

Dr. Dawson: What did Hasnat's parents say about you?

Princess Diana: There was a goddamn interview with Dr. Rashid Khan, Hasnat's father, in the *Daily Express*.

Dr. Dawson: What did he say?

Princess Diana: Hasnat's father said, "Hasnat is not going to marry Princess Diana... We're looking for a bride for him. She should be from a respectable family, be rich, and be upper-middle-class..."

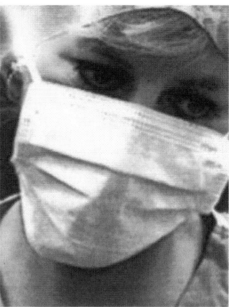

Princess Diana watched a heart operation as part of her romance with Hasnat Khan.

He wanted the girl to be from the Pathan tribe or at least be a Pakistani Muslim girl. My girlfriend warned me, "You keep barking up the wrong tree! You continue to bang your head into a wall."

Dr. Dawson: What happened next?

Princess Diana: I didn't tell him I was visiting his family. I flew to Pakistan and used the fund-raising project for the cancer hospital as my cover. I dropped in on Hasnat's family in Lahore.

Dr. Dawson: How did it go?

Princess Diana is arriving at the Royal Brompton National Heart and Lung Hospital, where Dr. Khan worked.

Princess Diana: I bloody knocked myself out. I charmed his parents, and we took photos with his family and relatives. I sat with the children watching cartoons on TV. But Hasnat's mother was adamant that he was going to marry a nice Pakistani Muslim girl.

Dr. Dawson: How did Hasnat react?

Princess Diana: Hasnat was very upset. I called him 20 times a day to fix it. I wanted to get his hospital administrators to change his schedule so we could take a long holiday abroad. His long hours did not leave enough time for us to be together.

A friend told me: "Why are you stalking his family uninvited? Because his parents did not welcome you as their future daughter-in-law. How did harassing him on the phone work?"

Dr. Dawson: What was your next strategy to get Hasnat to love you?

Princess Diana: In Italy, I met Dr. Christian Barnard, the heart-transplant doctor from South Africa. I invited Dr. Barnard to dinner at Kensington Palace and asked him to get Hasnat a position at a hospital in South Africa.

My thinking was that we could marry in South Africa and escape the press. But Hasnat was enraged when Dr. Barnard asked for his resume.

Dr. Dawson: Did this hit the press?

Princess Diana: The papers ran some articles that Hasnat and I were unofficially engaged after I met with his family in Pakistan.

Dr. Dawson: What happened next?

Princess Diana: Hasnat met me in Hyde Park at night. He told me our romance was over. I'm afraid I did not take it well. I was sobbing and yelling at him.

My girlfriend was blasting me: "You are acting like 'The One' was the last man on Earth. Listening to you, I feel like I'm hallucinating. You are the hottest, most desirable, most beautiful, most stylish royal princess in the world."

"You can get almost any man. Why do you keep chasing men you cannot have? Either they're married, or they're gold-digging playboys. You should be able to perceive if a man is an eligible guy. Why are you so needy and aggressive and desperate?"

Dr. Dawson: How does all this make you feel?

Princess Diana: When a man I love rejects me, I wish I was dead. A friend was trying to cheer me up and said, "Don't put yourself in a position where you'll be hurt and traumatized.

You can go to the next party, charity function, or social engagement and let your friends know you're available and looking for a new man."

Dr. Dawson: Okay.

Princess Diana: All I want to do when I break up with a man is to cry and play sad love songs.

A friend coached me, "The best medicine for you is to go out and get some attention from single men. You can combine your social engagements for humanitarian purposes and charity balls with your search for a new love. Remember, if God shuts one door, further down the hallway of life, your Higher Power will open another door or window for you."

14

Diana's last romance was with Dodi Fayed, a 42-year-old Egyptian Muslim who had opened a movie production company in Los Angeles. In this chapter, she continued discussing her love affairs.

Dr. Dawson: Why don't you tell me about this Dodi Fayed? How does he compare with Hasnat Khan?

Princess Diana: Hasnat was very private, intense, and dedicated to his medical career. Dodi Fayed was sort of casual and seeking to be famous.

Dodi worked for his father, who owned Harrods department store in London, and he had a film company in Los Angeles. He was the son of Egyptian Mohamed Al-Fayed.

A girlfriend warned me: "He's a cocaine addict and a playboy who throws parties several times a week at his Beverly Hills house."

Left: Princess Diana and Dodi Fayed aboard his yacht. Right: Prince William and his wife, Kate, yacht racing in New Zealand.

Dr. Dawson: How did you meet Dodi?

Princess Diana: Originally, I met him at a polo match in 1986. Prince Charles' polo team played the Fayed team. His father invited my boys and me to be his holiday guests in St Tropez, and I got to know Dodi then.

Dr. Dawson: I read that Dodi was 42, was married to a model for eight months, and was divorced from her. He was scheduled to marry another model – American Kelly Fisher - this summer. But then you appeared. Were you serious about him?

Princess Diana: After breaking up with Hasnat, I was just looking for a distraction, a good time for my boys and myself. I wasn't going to hide in some castle, sobbing my eyes out over my broken heart.

Kelly Fisher showed off the engagement ring she said Dodi Fayed gave her. Dodi, a playboy, was cheating on her with Princess Diana. Some tabloid papers reported Dodi cast her aside for Princess Diana.

A girlfriend told me: "Dodi seems like such a strange choice compared to Hasnat. He's got a track record of dating trophy women, including Julia Roberts, Brooke Shields, and now you. When he's in his house in Beverly Hills, he throws several parties a week for the Hollywood crowd."

"Dodi is a cocaine addict, a rich playboy, and drives Ferrari sports cars. His father supports him by giving him an allowance of $100,000 a month. Is there any other reason why you're dating him?"

Then she said, "You're just getting revenge against Hasnat by dating Dodi! You're trying to send a message to Hasnat, Prince Charles, and the British monarchy! Why are you dating a rich Muslim playboy?"

Left: Attorney Gloria Allred held the hand of model Kelly Fisher to display a sapphire engagement ring during a news conference in Los Angeles. Kelly was taking legal action against Dodi. Allred always seemed to be in the middle of sex and love affair scandals. Dodi's sudden death took the air out of her legal sails. Center: Prince Harry and Meghan Markle aboard the royal yacht. Right: Prince William and Kate's Seychelles honeymoon.

Dr. Dawson: Okay, go on.

Princess Diana: Hasnat broke up with me because he didn't want the public pressure and the press in his face. And since I'm not a Muslim woman from Pakistan, his family does not approve of me as a wife for him.

Hasnat was just an impossible dream. Hasnat is not the type to suddenly get jealous because I'm dating Dodi and marry me. Of course, the royals would not accept either Hasnat or Dodi.

Dr. Dawson: What's Dodi like?

Center: Diana and Dodi Al Fayed on a holiday escape on the French Riviera. Right: Prince William and Kate on vacation in Mustique, a tropical island in the Caribbean.

Princess Diana: He's a charming fellow. Dodi keeps showering me with gifts, and I don't like his conspicuous consumption. Hasnat either wanted to get sleep after a long shift at the hospital, or he'd do something simple like drink a beer and watch sports on TV. Dodi is the opposite and loves publicity, showing off with yachts, expensive cars, posh hotels, and mansions.

Dr. Dawson: Your divorce was completed on July 15th. I understand you've refused the royal security detail. In my opinion, that's a mistake. Since you're the most famous woman in the world, you need that extra professional protection. Why are you taking the risk with your security when you could have personal protection officers?

Left: Dodi Fayed and Princess Diana on the French Riviera. Right: Prince Harry and Meghan Markle enjoying the French Riviera.

Princess Diana: The royal security men are used as spies by the royal family. I don't want their noses in my business. Dodi and Mohamed Al Fayed have bodyguards, surveillance cameras, and protection.

One psychiatrist told me: "You're being paranoid, and you've got delusions of persecution. That's why you dropped your security detail."

Dr. Dawson: As I've told you, you're suffering from BPD syndrome – Borderline Personality Disorder. Impaired perception and reasoning and significantly volatile relationships – intense and unstable personal relationships – are part of BPD. You have to determine if your security is more essential than your suspicions about people spying or monitoring you.

Left: Princess Diana and Dodi Fayed on an escape along the French Riviera. Right: Prince William and Kate Middleton yachting off Ibiza, 2006.

Princess Diana: You think I'm too suspicious of the royal family? What other BPD symptoms do I have?

Dr. Dawson: I think you need professional police protection. I've told you to draw a line around yourself. Anything outside the circle is none of your business. Why do you care what the royals and their camp think of you?

You can't control them. Your safety and security are more central than any feedback royal protection officers might give them. Do you want to hear about your other BPD symptoms or characteristics?

Princess Diana: Yes.

Dr. Dawson: Two other areas have caused you problems. One is poorly regulated emotions. Another is impulsivity.

Left: Dodi Fayed on a date with Brooke Shields. Right: Prince Harry was simultaneously romancing an English model, Sarah Ann Macklin, and Meghan Markle.

Princess Diana: How are my emotions poorly regulated?

Dr. Dawson: As far as poorly regulated emotions, you have psychological issues in this area including mood swings, depression, temper tantrums, violent and volatile emotions, anxiety, inappropriate, intense anger, or inability to control anger, and chronic feelings of emptiness. Don't worry about it. We'll get back to your symptoms. I'll give you some self-help tips. Okay?

Princess Diana: Oh my god! I'm a psycho! What about impulsivity?

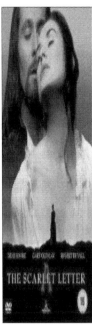

Dodi Fayed executive produced these movies: *Hook, The Scarlet Letter, Chariots of Fire,* and *FX.*

Dr. Dawson: Your impulsivity behavior includes self-destructive tendencies – you've had 4 or 5 suicide attempts, gestures or threats, and self-mutilating behavior. You've cut yourself several times.

Princess Diana: What about my eating disorder?

Dr. Dawson: Also, in this category is your eating disorder, which is now in remission – bulimia, bingeing, and purging. And in this impulsive category are a string of love affairs you've had.

I wouldn't call you promiscuous, but you're on the border of it. Either you'll overcome unstable relationships through psychotherapy or hit bottom after several breakups.

Left: Dodi Fayed was romancing Julia Roberts at a London film premiere. Julia was one of the stars of *Hook*, a film Dodi executive produced. Right: Prince Harry dating TV star Meghan Markle.

Princess Diana: What am I to do? Race into an insane asylum?

Dr. Dawson: You don't need a hospital. However, you need intensive psychotherapy on a long-term basis for your BPD. I can continue to help you.

Princess Diana: What's the answer to all these psychological symptoms?

Dr. Dawson: You can start by being aware that you are your own worst enemy. You need to get out of your way.

Paranoid feelings are not fact – they are unrealistic feelings. I'd strongly advise you to rethink refusing the royal security detail and get a personal protection officer.

Left: Princess Diana was exasperated by the paparazzi and media harassing her. Right: Diana working out in a gym, 1993.

Princess Diana: I'll think about it. What else? How do I avoid the wrong man and unstable relationships?

Dr. Dawson: You'll have stable love relationships naturally after you've worked through your conflicts in psychotherapy. But you can handle your negative symptoms with some self-help techniques at home by yourself. What's bothering you the most?

Princess Diana: I'm angry, restless, and frustrated. Because my romances keep hitting the rocks, and then the media blows it up in my face! What can I do, Dr. Dawson?

15

Princess Diana discussed issues related to her BPD symptoms in this chapter.

Dr. Dawson: Can you review some issues and see if we can see an underlying pattern? How prepared were you for the pressures that came with marrying into the Royal Family?

Princess Diana: I was only 19. Like a lot of teenagers, I thought I was ready for anything. Why should I worry? I had Prince Charles in my corner.

Dr. Dawson: What did you expect from marriage to Prince Charles?

Left: Princess Diana and Prince Charles in 1985. Right: Prince William, Prince Harry, Meghan, and Kate, 2019.

Princess Diana: I was afraid I was stuck in the same rut my parents were in, which led to their divorce. I was determined to work hard to overcome any marriage problems. I was desperate to avoid being abandoned by Prince Charles.

Dr. Dawson: Now that we've discussed your BPD (Borderline Personality Disorder), do you see any BPD symptoms so far?

Princess Diana: I'm afraid I don't have a clue. Doctor, please enlighten me.

Dr. Dawson: Remember when we were discussing how you were minimizing Prince Charles' negative behavior both before and after you were married?

Left: Shown are Prince Philip, the Queen, Prince Charles, and Princess Diana on the balcony of Buckingham Palace after their wedding. Right: The royal family on the balcony of Buckingham Palace, 2019.

Princess Diana: Charles did not call me when I was in Australia and did not take or return my calls. When I got back somebody from his office sent me some flowers without a note – Charles did not send them.

Dr. Dawson: What happened when he proposed to you?

Princess Diana: Charles made some insincere sounding, mushy, syrupy, and saccharine comments about how much he missed me. Then he blurted out, "Will you marry me?" I thought he was joking because it was so sudden and not organic. There was no development of affection and love.

Left: Queen Elizabeth II, Prince Charles, the Queen Mother, and Princess Diana at Buckingham Palace. Right: Royal family, 2019.

Dr. Dawson: Prince Philip and the Queen had pressured Charles to hurry up and marry a naïve virgin of noble birth. The Firm wanted Charles and you to have a marriage of convenience, produce heirs, and the royals arranged it. How did you see it then?

Princess Diana: I told myself we were in love. And I made excuses for Charles when he was inconsistent with my romantic view of him.

Dr. Dawson: If you'll recall what we discussed about BPD, it is a Borderline Personality Disorder symptom to have black-and-white perceptions of people.

Left: Princess Diana and Camilla. Right: Kate Middleton and Meghan Markle.

BPD people usually idealize people or later demonize them because they have unrealistic standards for people. You knew before you married Prince Charles that he was involved in a sex affair with Camilla. How did you handle all this cognitive dissonance?

Princess Diana: I agree I was idealizing Charles and I minimized the negatives at the time.

Dr. Dawson: You said you "desperately" wanted it to work, and you "desperately" loved Charles. What do you think was driving that?

Pictured are Diana, Charles, Camilla, a romantic triangle.

Princess Diana: Because my parents were divorced, I want a happy marriage.

Dr. Dawson: You felt abandoned as a child when your parents split, and your mother left. A key factor with BPD people is that they make frantic efforts to avoid real or imagined abandonment. You were desperate to avoid abandonment and willing to accept Camilla, being ignored, and inconsiderate behavior on Charles's part.

Princess Diana: I'd have to agree. I think my fears of abandonment have driven me to some difficult situations.

Dr. Dawson: What's your view on becoming the Princess of Wales and maybe Queen?

Left: Princess Diana and Princess Grace. Right: Prince Harry and Princess Charlene of Monaco.

Princess Diana: I was too naïve to be afraid of the challenge. I did not expect to be Queen. I was misinformed about the media. I was told the press would be discreet and stay quietly out of our way.

The media pressure was the opposite and overwhelming. I was on the front page of the papers daily. They put me up on some perfectionistic pedestal. Then the only way to go was down.

Dr. Dawson: How did you handle it as you morphed from Lady Diana Spencer to the most famous woman in the world, Princess Diana? How did it feel?

Left: Diana wanted to be more than an English Barbie doll with a royal princess crown. Right: Kate Middleton, Meghan Markle.

Princess Diana: I was astonished that people would be so incredibly curious about me. I assumed it was because of Prince Charles' fame. It seemed like I was becoming a product people could use to make money, like an English Barbie doll with a royal princess crown.

Dr. Dawson: What was your response to frantic and feverish attention from crowds of people and the press? What impulsive responses were you making to this pressure behind the scenes?

Pictured is Diana, Princess of Wales, seven months pregnant in Scilly Isles in April 1984. Behind the scenes, she battled an eating disorder. The Princess of Wales looked too thin (center), which was a result of her eating disorder. Charles and Diana met Barry Manilow. Right: Prince Charles meets the Spice Girls.

Princess Diana: I was suffering from my eating disorder – bulimia, bingeing, and purging - vomiting my food.

Dr. Dawson: What happened when you were pregnant?

Princess Diana: I was doubly sick with morning sickness vomiting combined with bulimia – overeating and then vomiting it up.

Left to right: Prince Charles, Princess Diana, Prince William, Kate, Prince Harry, Meghan.

Dr. Dawson: What about self-injuring behavior?

Princess Diana: When I didn't get attention from Charles, I cut myself in various places and was bleeding. It disgusted Charles, and he said, "You are just crying wolf."

Dr. Dawson: What about suicidal behavior?

Princess Diana: I made several suicide attempts and even threw myself down a staircase. It made Charles angry, and the Queen was shocked.

Dr. Dawson: Frequently, BPD sufferers show impulsive symptoms such as eating disorders, self-injury, and suicide attempts. It sounds like your adjustment to being the Princess of Wales was a disaster.

Left: Princess Diana is shaking hands with a crowd on a Royal Tour of Canada in 1986. Right: Prince William and Kate Middleton on a Royal Tour of Canada.

Were you isolated and left alone to handle being Princess Diana? Was that what happened?

Princess Diana: The problem was that the media, with the paparazzi, were all over. I symbolized some royal-fairy tale which people had read about as children. Everybody wanted the happy, fairy-tale ending. So I had to endure the trial-and-error process.

Dr. Dawson: How did it all start again?

Left: Princess Diana and Prince Charles on a 1983 Royal Tour of Australia. Right: Prince Harry and Meghan meet crowds in Australia.

Princess Diana: We took a tour of Australia, and I was high-pressured to perform like a trained seal in coping with crowds of strangers by Prince Charles and the press. I told Charles, "I can't cope with this bloody public relations nonsense!" He ordered me to go through the motions and press the flesh – meet endless crowds of strangers.

I was very traumatized by meeting thousands of strangers for six weeks in Australia and New Zealand. It was like diving into a freezing tank of water to learn my royal duty, facing the crowds of strangers, and adapting to the media endlessly snapping my photo and videotaping me. It was so unbelievably demanding.

Dr. Dawson: How bad was the pressure of meeting the public and facing the press when you started?

Left: Pictured is Diana on a 1983 New Zealand tour. The Prince and Princess of Wales go on a walkabout in Perth, Western Australia (center). Right: Prince Harry and Meghan Markle toured Australia, New Zealand.

Princess Diana: I was out of my mind with anxiety. Because my self-image was terrible. I saw myself as this fat slob who was 19 to 21 years-of-age. Why would anybody be interested in a chubby 20-year-old kid? Granted, I was suddenly, Princess Diana. But in my mind, I was nothing special.

Dr. Dawson: Were you happy early in your marriage?

Princess Diana: I was naïve enough to think I was happily married at times. But, of course, Camilla was always jumping into bed with Charles. Add to that the pressure from the media.

Left: Prince Charles and Princess Diana on an Australian tour. Right: Prince Harry and Meghan Markle greeted crowds on an Australian tour.

Then Charles became exasperated. He was jealous of the attention I was getting. Nobody in Australia or New Zealand among the crowds wanted to see him. Everybody was yelling to see the Princess of Wales. His pride was hurt.

Dr. Dawson: You were asked if the press coverage of you was flattering. Was it?

Princess Diana: The press attention only made Charles mad when it focused on me. Mix in Camilla plus the media pressure, and it was soon hell.

Dr. Dawson: We talked about four of the major groups of symptoms in BPD: poorly regulated emotions, impulsivity, impaired perception and reasoning, and markedly disturbed relationships. Can you see your poorly controlled emotions?

Left: A pleased public gazed with pleasure on the Prince and pregnant Princess of Wales during their walkabout in St. Mary's on the Scilly Isles. Center/left: Screaming crowds met Prince Harry and Meghan Markle on their tours of Australia, New Zealand, and Fiji. Meghan was a favorite of the massive crowds, similar to Princess Diana's experience.

Princess Diana: My poorly regulated emotions? Well, I was freaked-out meeting all those strangers.

Dr. Dawson: Not just freaked-out, but you refused to go over and talk to people in the crowds. Charles demanded it. You had mood swings, depression, anxiety, and chronic feelings of emptiness. What about your impaired perception and reasoning?

Left: Princess Diana experienced anxiety coping with meeting crowds of strangers on tour while pregnant. Right: Prince Harry and Meghan Markle greeted excited crowds on Australian, New Zealand, and Fiji tours.

Princess Diana: I perceived I was not up to interfacing with all those crowds of strangers.

Dr. Dawson: I see flashes of your paranoid thinking, maybe loss of contact with reality at times, and perhaps some delusions of persecution. You felt people didn't like you, maybe were out to get you, or even hurt you. How did your unstable self-image or sense of self show up then?

Princess Diana: I was very insecure.

Diana visited Westonbirt School in Tetbury, Gloucestershire on July 19, 1985 (left). Princess Diana during a Royal tour of New Zealand (center). Right: Meghan Markle greeted and charmed crowds in Australia and New Zealand. Prince Harry and Meghan were a big hit on tour.

Dr. Dawson: Yes, and you even remarked that you perceived yourself as unattractive – fat, chubby, and just 20 to 21 years old. Why would anybody want to see you? Your shaky self-concept was connected to your wild mood swings.

You've bounced from depression to almost mania. Your self-esteem and self-worth were near zero and were a function of approval from your husband. How did this impact your relationship with Charles?

Princess Diana: He was jealous when the crowds wanted to see me and not him. And when the press focused on me.

Dr. Dawson: Right. This was the start of you demonizing Charles in that he was jealous of you. When you had other impulsive symptoms like eating disorders, self-injury cutting, and suicide attempts, the process of demonizing Charles continued.

Finally, it justified you having lovers just like Charles had Camilla. Your relationship with Charles went from bad to worse. But enough psychobabble. What issues can you address with some self-help suggestions?

Princess Diana: Because of my romantic conflicts, I've been depressed, lonely, and sad.

P.196 — Prince Harry
P.179

Printed in Great Britain
by Amazon